THE OFFICIAL GUIDE

Printed in the UK by MPG Books, Bodmin

Published by: Sanctuary Publishing Limited, 45-53 Sinclair Road, London
W14 0NS, United Kingdom

www.sanctuarypublishing.com

Copyright: Michael Prochak, 2002

Cover artwork courtesy of Steinberg Media Technologies AG

ISBN: 1-86074-470-2

THE OFFICIAL GUIDE

MICHAEL PROCHAK

Sanctuary

This one is for the usual crew out there in search of the lost discordian.

'I believe that instinct is what makes a genius a genius.'
- Bob Dylan

'No limits allowed, no limits exist.'
- John Lily

contents

CHAPTER 7

CHAPTER 8

CHAPTER 9

CHAPTER 10

introduction and overview

For practising musicians, producers and enthusiasts, Cubase has become one of the best-known music-production applications available throughout the world. In many ways, it's hard to believe that Cubase started life on the humble Atari ST platform back in 1989, and that it wasn't until it was released for the Macintosh and Windows as a MIDI sequencer that it really began to blossom. Although by 1996 the idea of a MIDI-and-audio sequencer had established itself in the digital music arena, Steinberg's Macintosh release of Cubase VST added a new definition of 'big and clever' with the inclusion of real-time effects and EQ, all neatly packaged within the now-familiar sequencer environment, without the use of additional DSP hardware.

Steinberg's latest release of this popular application, Cubase SX, represents a totally new generation in music-creation and -production software tools. Steinberg has spent more than 15 years creating the tools that musicians want to use, and all the best and latest technology is crammed into this all-new edition, Cubase SX. With SX's forerunners, Steinberg proved that, in an increasingly digital environment, there is no compelling need to keep shelling out for expensive and constantly out-of-date dedicated audio hardware in order to create extremely capable and creative audio workstations. Most users will find that Cubase SX is not just equal to most other available digital systems, but that it's one which, for a lot of musicians and producers, can actually be better, more comfortable and certainly more flexible. For example, Cubase SX comes complete with VST System Link, allowing several computers to be linked together and actually perform as one fully integrated system. This means that the idea of a maximum (read 'limited') project size simply doesn't apply any more. And it doesn't stop there.

As you get acquainted with Cubase SX, you'll find myriad advantages that give you unprecedented freedom to work in the way that you, the musician, really want to work. Features range from advanced automated mixing facilities with support for VST 2.0 plug-ins and virtual instruments and ASIO 2.0-compatible audio hardware to extremely flexible multiple undo and redo options, giving you the facility to selectively remove or modify applied audio processing at any point in the data's history. You have complete surround-sound support and handling that makes other systems look like such a facility was some sort of afterthought rather than an integral part of the initial design goal. Clearly, Cubase SX is decidedly better than most of its wannabe competitors. The Cubase SX development team has obviously benefited immensely from the input they've received from users – the people actually working with Cubase in their professional lives or as music enthusiasts.

overview

So what's new and different in Cubase SX? Well, basically, *everything*. Cubase SX is not merely an updated version of Cubase VST; it has been completely redesigned from the inside out. Fortunately, most of this is totally transparent to the user, and all of the main working areas of the program are still very similar to earlier versions. However, there are various changes in how recorded files are handled, there are changes in terminology used and the main menu structure is different, along with other cosmetic developments. But while these changes might make things slightly confusing initially to users of previous versions of Cubase, in the long run the advantages they provide make them all worthwhile.

what's different in SX?

Although Steinberg has created a completely new application with the release of SX, to experienced Cubase users a lot of the look and feel remains the same, just a lot slicker and perhaps even a bit more intuitive. However, there are a number of distinct differences in SX that set it apart from previous versions of Cubase. These include:

Songs And Arrangements
Unlike Cubase VST, in SX the basic concept of songs and arrangements is no longer used. Instead, the native document format a 'project' (extension .cpr) is used, and all settings and file references relating to the project are stored in the Project folder, which is designated when you create a project. You can have several open projects, but only one can be active at any one time. You can, of course, work with multiple arrangements in the same way as on previous versions of Cubase, since several projects can share the same Project folder. However, having different formats for songs and arrangements is redundant since you can now simply create new projects and assign them to the same Project folder.

Project Window Versus Arrange Window
Cubase SX's main working area, the Project window, is pretty much the same as the Arrange window in earlier versions of Cubase. This area allows for real-time placement of audio, video and MIDI parts and the performing of almost

all primary editing tasks, including automation, as well as giving you an overview of an entire project. However, you will notice that Cubase SX uses different terminology to earlier Cubase versions for referencing audio files in a project.

Audio Channels

In the new version of SX, you don't have to specify the number of audio channels to use in a project, nor do you have to designate an audio channel to record on; you can simply create as many audio tracks as you feel you need in any project, a number limited only by what your computer can handle. For convenience, in Cubase SX an audio track and an audio channel are the same thing and all audio tracks will have a corresponding audio-channel strip in the Mixer.

Recording Audio

In earlier versions of Cubase, recording normally took place on the track that was selected. In Cubase SX, however, you simply have to activate the Record Enable button for each track on which you wish to record. The number of tracks on which you can record at a time depends on the number of activated inputs on your audio hardware. You can also set things up so that, on selected tracks, Record Enable is activated automatically.

Events And Parts

In Cubase SX, audio events can appear directly on audio tracks in the Project window, so there is no longer any need for audio parts. You can also put one or several audio events into an audio part, which is particularly useful when it comes to grouping events together and moving them all as one unit.

Dynamic Events

Sorry, there are no dynamic events for audio events any more. Instead, you now need to use the regular automation features to automate volume and pan. The matchpoints feature in previous versions of Cubase has also been replaced by a comprehensive hitpoint-editing feature.

Applying Processing

In Cubase SX, you can of course still use plug-in effects in real time, but you can now also permanently apply the effect processing to selected audio events.

MIDI-related differences

Recording MIDI

As I said, in previous versions of Cubase, MIDI recording normally happened on a selected track, whereas in Cubase SX you can record on all tracks that are record enabled and also set things up so that selected tracks are automatically record enabled. Unlike the MIDI input in previous versions, which was a global setting for all tracks, in Cubase SX tracks can be set separately for each MIDI track.

Setting MIDI Thru
In order to be able to play a connected MIDI instrument in Cubase SX, MIDI Thru must first be activated, which is now achieved either by record-enabling the track or by clicking the track's Monitor button.

Editing MIDI
In previous versions of Cubase, you could select a MIDI track in the Track list and open it in a MIDI editor. In Cubase SX, you need to select one or several parts on the track before you can open a MIDI editor.

Play Parameters
Cubase SX now extends considerably the potential for real-time processing of MIDI data and comes with a number of MIDI effect plug-ins capable of transforming the MIDI output from a track in various ways. However, unlike the Play parameters in previous versions, Track parameters in Cubase SX cannot be applied to individual MIDI parts. Instead, they are always set up for complete MIDI tracks.

Drum Tracks
Unlike previous incarnations, there is no longer a specific track class for drums. Instead, you can assign a drum map to any MIDI track. This will give you the same drum-editing features as in previous Cubase versions.

Mixing
Mixing MIDI is now done in the Track Mixer, along with your audio channels. The MIDI channel strips are similar to the channel strips in the MIDI Track Mixer, allowing you to set levels, panning and other parameters for your MIDI tracks.

what's completely new in Cubase SX?

At the risk of sounding repetitive, it can't be over-emphasised that Cubase SX is a completely rewritten application built on the foundations and technology of Steinberg's aristocratic Nuendo. As a bit of useless information, you might like to know that the SX tag was added to reinforce the complete rebirth of this application and, perhaps more prosaically, was named after Essex by its developers as the codename for the project, for some reason. (I suppose we should just be grateful that the development team had never heard of Scunthorpe!) Since SX is a completely new incarnation of Cubase, it's worth glancing through the list of totally new features before you get stuck into any serious production work. Powerful new features and functionality include:

Multiple Undo And Redo

Cubase SX offers an all-singing, all-dancing, wide-ranging multiple Undo facility which, as it says on the tin, allows you to undo virtually any action you perform.

Edit History

The Edit History dialog now allows you to undo or redo several actions in one go.

Offline Process History

The Offline Process History allows you to remove and modify applied processing. This is actually different from the 'regular' Undo function in that you don't have to undo processing functions in the order that they were performed.

Graphic Editing Of Automation Events

Automation handling has also been greatly improved in Cubase SX. Automation events can now be drawn graphically in the Project window, and each audio and MIDI track in the Track list has an automation track containing all parameters for each selected track. You can select which parameters to view and edit by opening subtracks for the automation track. You can also, of course, use normal Write and Read automation to record your actions, just as you could in previous versions of Cubase. On top of that, all effect control panels also feature Write and Read buttons and each automated effect and VST instrument has its own automation track in the Track list, with subtracks for each parameter.

Surround Sound

Cubase SX has introduced integrated surround-sound features with support for several popular formats.

Integration

The newly crafted graphic design in Cubase SX integrates all of the various windows in a much clearer way than in previous versions – for example, the Inspector, the Track list and the Track Mixer have many shared parameters which all use the same style of buttons, allowing you to alter a range of settings quickly and intuitively in whichever window you're currently working.

Hitpoints

Hitpoint editing is a new feature of the Sample Editor which allows you to create 'slices' of data to be used in drum loops, or indeed those of any instrument. A sliced loop can then adapt to changes in tempo without its pitch being affecting. The previous system of using tempo- and time-based hitpoints for matching time and metre positions, found in Cubase VST, is no longer used.

VST System Link

This is a new system for networking computers using VST software and ASIO (Audio Stream Input/Output) hardware allowing you to work with multiple computers (including cross-platform systems) and to dedicate certain tasks to different computers. For example, you could run all VST instruments on one computer, all audio tracks on another and so on.

summary

Writing a book that explains every aspect of every feature in a program like Cubase SX would be a thankless and, to be quite honest, futile task. Since music doesn't consist of a single genre, the requirements of all musicians can't be generalised or anticipated in a single volume. As a practising musician or producer, the type or style of music that you wish to produce will ultimately dictate which features and functions and precisely how much of Cubase SX's power you will actually want or need to use. As it happens, I tend to consider myself a musician and composer first and a producer second, which is why this book – although hopefully as comprehensive as possible for a fast guide – is designed primarily to introduce practising musicians, in particular, to the skills and techniques required to use the essential elements of Cubase SX, whether they've read the manual or not. It's also designed specifically for musicians and producers who traditionally hate manuals and prefer a more heuristic approach, dipping into features and functionality as and when the need arises. Basically, the idea is to familiarise you with the essence of Cubase SX so that you're free to create the music you hear in your head but have, perhaps, been unable to realise in a recorded form...until now.

Cubase is such a mind-bogglingly massive application that, for the purposes of this book, I will assume that you have at least a familiarity with the inner workings of your PC and at least a reasonable familiarity with Cubase VST. I've also not gone into a lot of technical detail concerning add-on audio cards or peripherals, since these will vary considerably depending on your own personal studio set-up. However, when it comes to add-ons and MIDI devices, I can't recommend strongly enough that you actually read the manuals and documentation. Yes, it *is* boring, but in these instances it's the only hope you have of getting everything working together in a reasonably harmonious fashion.

If you're at all like me, you believe that music is magic, and ultimately the magic of music creation always depends on something totally indefinable, something that turns a riff, a break or a chord sequence into something transcendental. Sometimes it's hard work and good intentions, but sometimes it's serendipity or dumb luck. As it happens, a good digital-audio workstation running Cubase SX really can cater for nearly all of your creative-recording studio needs, but you still have to remember that it won't write your songs for you and it doesn't come with creativity and talent plug-ins. As clever and as powerful as this technology might be, it's worth reflecting on the notion that, for the most part, musical perfection does not exist. And even if it did, a MIDI-plus-audio sequencer, no matter how powerful and accessible, is not what you should be using to search for it. As you'll see through reading this book, some level of technical involvement is inevitable, and you'll need to browse the manual and peripheral documentation that comes with the program, at least. And to get the most out of Cubase SX, you'll also have to consider things like microphones, monitors, effects, room acoustics, tuning and all the other stuff you'd usually have to think about in any other recording environment. That's why the real secret for musicians and producers alike is simply to know the limits of the software, however few they might be, and to be properly equipped before taking the musical plunge. Luckily, with Steinberg's Cubase SX, you have the freedom and ability to choose just how deeply you wish or, more importantly, need to go. When you're working with any digital equipment, it's worth reminding yourself on a regular basis that, just because you can, it doesn't mean you should. Sure, the user interface and level of functionality can always be adapted to each individual's personal needs and preferences, but somewhere along the line it's you, the musician, who needs to know how to enhance that power and add the essential element of magic.

first steps

At this moment in time, Cubase SX is available only for the Windows platform, and even then you're going to require a pretty heavy-duty system running Windows 2000 or XP to handle the torque. Like it or not, Cubase SX is formally unsupported, if not totally, and probably completely incompatible with systems running Windows 9x, ME or NT. So, if you've got a PC running any of those earlier systems, stop reading now and go out and upgrade your kit. As well as an up-to-date version of Windows, you'll also need a PC with at least one USB port, which shouldn't pose too much of a problem these days. Steinberg maintain that, by not supporting 'legacy' systems, they've been able to provide a better product by focusing on newer technology to improve performance. However, for a lot of potential users, this does mean spending more money.

The minimum requirements for running Cubase SX are a lot more strict than with previous versions, and you won't be able to get anywhere without at least a 500MHz Pentium III with a minimum of 256Mb of RAM. Since this sort of spec is fairly typical of more modern PCs sold with Windows XP, this also shouldn't pose much of a problem, unless you're still running vintage kit. You should also ensure that your display has a resolution of no less than 1,024 x 768. Certain windows in Cubase SX need at least this much space just to be fully visible, and of course two screens are always better than one, if you can afford them.

The main reason why you'll need a free USB port is because Steinberg, in its infinite wisdom, uses a dongle as a security device. With Cubase SX, this plugs into a USB port and replaces the previous parallel-port device which caused so many disruptive hassle for PC users when Cubase VST version 5 was first released.

I have to go on record at this point to say that I hate dongles and think they're a dreadfully intrusive method of copy protection which will always play havoc with your system in one way or another. In a word, they suck. As a Mac user, I never had to suffer the indignities of a dongle with Cubase VST 5, and it's my opinion that Steinberg could have come up with a better and less intrusive security option for the PC as well. OK, piracy is a problem, but the reality is that cracked versions of Cubase SX were available on the net when the application was still in its beta stages, and even before its general worldwide release cracked versions with dongle bypasses were also available. So why use a security mechanism that doesn't fully protect the application and yet has the potential to cause seriously annoying problems for legitimate users who have actually paid good money for the program? But, as I said, that's only my opinion.

Early comments from Steinberg suggested that this new dongle could also be used to store additional data for other product authorisation. So, for example, at some point in time you could find that you needed it to provide copy-protection information for all of your plug-in instruments and effects, which (again, depending on your point of view) could be seen as a blessing or a curse if and/or when it decides to pack up in the course of your recording or mixing. As a concession to customer loyalty, Steinberg has allowed users of Cubase VST version 5 to keep their original dongles when upgrading, and both applications generally seem to co-exist on the same machine. Oh yes, and you always have to remember that the dongle needs to be plugged into the computer's USB port after installing Cubase SX and restarting the computer. If you plug it in first, you'll probably experience a few recognition problems. When the dongle is plugged into the USB port, Windows will automatically register it as a new hardware device and will attempt to find drivers for it. As you might expect, these necessary drivers won't be there until Cubase SX has been installed and the computer has been restarted.

installing SX and setting up your system

Before you do anything else, you should set up your specific audio hardware and its drivers. There are a lot of options available for soundcards, so suffice it to say that you'll need to install your chosen card and related equipment in your particular PC, following the card's instructions. Once you've done this, you'll need to install the particular driver specified for the card. There are three types of drivers that could apply: card-specific ASIO drivers, DirectX drivers and common Windows Multimedia drivers

ASIO Driver
If your soundcard has a specific ASIO driver, it will most likely be included with the card itself. However, you should always check the card manufacturer's website for the most recent drivers and updates. And I know that this can be a drag, but you'll need to refer to the manufacturer's instructions for details on how to install the driver.

DirectX Driver
If your audio card is DirectX compatible, its DirectX drivers will most likely be installed when you install the card, as is also the case with the ubiquitous Windows

Multimedia driver. If you've downloaded special DirectX drivers for the audio card, you should once again follow the manufacturer's installation instructions.

Windows Multimedia Driver

This driver is fairly common and is normally included with all types of regular PC audio cards, and some such drivers are even included with Windows itself. The method of the audio card's installation depends on whether it's 'plug-and-play compatible'. If it is, Windows will detect the card once it's plugged in and will ask for the necessary driver disks. If not, you'll need to use the 'Add New Hardware' control panels to install the card and its drivers. And again, it might be boring, but you'll still have to refer to the documentation that comes with the card. If, for whatever reason, you find yourself with an audio card but no driver, be sure to check the manufacturer's website or ask your music or computer dealer for help.

To make sure that the audio card works as expected, you can run two simple tests. Firstly, use any software included with the audio card to make sure that you can record and play back audio without any problems. Secondly, if your card is accessed via a standard Windows driver, use the Media Player application included with Windows to play back an audio file. If this works, you know your card is installed properly.

installing a MIDI interface

In order to use MIDI, you'll need at least one MIDI interface, at least one MIDI instrument and some sort of audio equipment over which to listen to the sound generated by your gear. Although working with MIDI can appear somewhat arcane, installation instructions for a MIDI interface are normally included with the product, although you might find that a degree of trial and error and experimentation is necessary when installing devices. Generally, you'll need to install the interface or MIDI synthesiser card inside your computer or physically connect it to a port on your PC, depending on which type of interface you have. If your interface has a power supply and/or a power switch, turn it on - you should then be able to install the interface's driver as described in the accompanying documentation. It's likely that you'll need a CD-ROM or - shock, horror! - a floppy disk, which should be supplied by the manufacturer of the MIDI interface, and you'll probably have to play mix-and-match with your cable connections as well.

hardware requirements

PC

As mentioned briefly earlier on, the absolute minimum requirements for running Cubase SX on a PC include a 500MHz Pentium III processor with 256Mb of RAM or an equivalent AMD processor. Steinberg's recommended configuration for optimum performance includes a 1GHz or faster dual Pentium III/Athlon processor with 512Mb of RAM, and as always in this department, more is better.

RAM

If you've ever done any work with audio, you'll know that it requires literally shedloads of RAM. In fact, there is a direct correlation between the amount of available RAM and the number of audio channels that you can have running at any one time. Like I said, 256Mb is the minimum requirement, but again size does matter and bigger really is better, and this is true of RAM just as it is of storage.

Hard-Disk Size

The size of your hard disk determines how many minutes of audio you'll be able to record. Believe it or not, recording one minute of stereo-CD-quality audio requires around 10Mb of hard-disk space. This means that eight stereo tracks in Cubase SX use up at least 80Mb of disk space per recording minute. And while Cubase is still generally seen as being an excellent MIDI sequencer, I can vouch for its equally excellent audio capabilities. My last album, which consisted of only acoustic audio and vocal tracks, was produced and mastered entirely on Cubase and still retains a warm, well-rounded, mellow sound.

It's also worth pointing out that the speed of your hard drive also determines the number of audio tracks that you can run at once. Known as *sustained transfer rate*, the quantity of information that the disk can read is reliant on the speed of your drive – and once again, more is good, while a lot more is even better.

Wheel Mouse

While a normal, run-of-the-mill mouse will work perfectly well with Cubase SX, Steinberg recommend the use of a wheel mouse, as they're convinced that this will considerably speed up value-editing and scrolling. Since I didn't have access to a wheel mouse when writing this book, I'll just have to take their word for it. However, like everything else to do with Cubase SX, your own personal working practices and musical requirements will determine the minutiae of how you set up your system.

installing Cubase SX

Installing Cubase SX is a pleasantly painless exercise. All you have to do is insert the CD-ROM, follow the prompts that appear onscreen, plug in your dongle and, as they say, Bob's your uncle – and since I actually have an

Uncle Bob, the whole process was even easier! If, as is generally the case these days, you're connected to the internet, the installation program will even contact Steinberg to check on any available updates, patches and fixes and give you the option of downloading and installing them. (It's also worth running this utility from time to time after installation to ensure that you've got the latest version of the software and any necessary fixes.) As I mentioned earlier, it's important that you remember to plug in the dongle after you've completed the installation procedure and you've restarted your computer. After you've done this, when you open the Windows Start menu, you'll find a Cubase SX group in the Programs submenu containing the following items.

Documentation
From the Programs submenu, you can access the 'Getting Started', 'Operation Manual' and 'Score Layout And Printing' documentation in the Acrobat .pdf format. Unfortunately, you don't get a printed manual with SX, and if you want a hard-copy reference you'll have to spend a bit more cash on printer cartridges. As you're reading this book, though, forget about printing out the manual; just refer to the .pdf documentation if you get bogged down in the details. (Incidentally, these documents are also available in the Help menu from within the program.)

ASIO DirectX Full Duplex Setup
This is the dialog box where you can choose your settings if your audio hardware uses DirectX drivers for audio playback and recording.

ASIO Multimedia Setup
This opens a dialog box in which you can choose settings for your ASIO system, which, if you're using the ASIO MME driver, handles audio recording and playback in Cubase SX. You can also open this dialog from within Cubase SX itself.

Cubase SX
This command does exactly what it says on the tin and, as you might expect, launches the actual program. You might also notice some additional items present here such as 'Read Me' files available on the Start menu. Even if you hate manuals, it's probably a good idea to read these files before you go about launching Cubase SX, as they might contain additional information not included in the manuals.

LCC
This item shows all SyncroSoft protection devices and the usual boring valid licences currently installed.

a word on soundcards

When it comes to soundcards, Steinberg recommends the use of any audio hardware that supports the ASIO protocol in order to ensure low latency values and trouble-free operation. Since most soundcard manufacturers have adapted to this standard and provide drivers for all of the latest operating systems, finding a suitable soundcard for your particular system shouldn't be difficult. Generally speaking, unless you try to run SX on an under-powered machine and a crappy Soundblaster-style soundcard, you won't encounter any major problems. It's also worth pointing out that Cubase SX doesn't provide any input-level adjustment for audio, since this is performed differently for each card. Adjusting input levels is done either in a special application included with the hardware or possibly from its ASIO control panel.

studio configurations

There are a variety of ways of configuring your studio set-up, depending on your requirements and preferences, the style of music you're producing and your production and individual working practices. Since I work primarily on a Mac, I was able to create this book with the help of Piotr (e-manuel) Dorosz, who engineered and co-produced my last album, which was recorded in part at Tonic Studios in Hastings. Obviously, the hardware configuration for the studio might be somewhat posher than the average home system, but it does give you an idea of the sort of power you'll need if you really want to push Cubase SX to the limits. The newest custom-built computer set-up that we used to evaluate Cubase SX essentially consisted of the following:

• Radeon 9700 Atlantis Pro (ATI Radeon 9700 Pro chipset, 128Mb DDR, 325/310, DVI, TVO)

• Intel Pentium 4 2.53GHz (533MHz) Northwood processor, 512k cache

• Thermaltake A1358 18" ATA133 round cable

• Maxtor 6Y080L0 DiamondMax Plus9 80GB UDMA133 (for audio)

• IBM 120GB UDMA 100 (for OS)

• Pioneer DVD-106S

• Crucial 512Mb 184-pin DIMM PC2100 DDR RAM, non-parity CL2.5 (times three = 1.5Gb RAM)

- Abit BD7-II-RAID motherboard

- Yamaha CRW-F1E-VK

- Windows 2000 Professional

- Cubase SX 1.03

- Hammerfall RME HDSP Multiface with PCI card

- ADSL 512kbs

- Networked 100 Fast Ethernet with three other PCs

- Two 19" flat-panel TFT iiyama monitors

- Creative Labs Soundblaster Live! (for system sounds and SoundFont playback)

- Quiet aluminium PC case, power-supply unit and removable hard-drive enclosure

In view of the above, sticking to Steinberg's minimum specs will still provide you with an excellent recording and production environment. However, aspiration is good, I'm told, and obviously the more powerful system you can afford to use, the more power you can wrench from Cubase SX.

chapter 2

getting started

With the magic of Cubase SX and a reasonable PC, musicians now have access to a fully integrated virtual recording studio that can be used to record, mix, edit and process MIDI and audio with equal professionalism. Like all modern sequencers, Cubase SX uses a sophisticated graphic interface that allows blocks of sound or MIDI information to be copied, sliced and moved around, while audio and MIDI recordings are visible within the same window to make editing and tracking easier by showing you exactly where your audio sources are in relation to your MIDI data. With the addition of VST (Virtual Studio Technology), Cubase and a few add-ons can easily cater for nearly all of your recording and production needs. OK, if you're a fanatical audio purist or an anal-retentive techie geek, you'll always be able to find something that's not absolutely perfect with various recordings, whether they're done on a PC at home or in a commercial studio, but as the *I Ching* says, perseverance furthers, and if you know your music and know the sound you want, Cubase SX is more than capable of helping you achieve that special blend you're after.

Having the best-equipped studio with obscenely expensive microphones, desks and effects would, like winning the lottery, be a wonderful solution in an ideal world, but most musicians don't live in such a world and rarely win the lottery. And in the real world, where you're more likely to be hit by an asteroid than win the lottery, even expensive, state-of-the-art studios still churn out a lot of well-produced yet ear-numbing mediocrity like the detritus spawned from *PopStars*, *Pop Idol* and the under-worked imaginations involved in their conception. And yes, even most of the self-obsessed digital dance culture reflects the dangers of good technology that can semi-automatically produce the same democratically mundane effects and styles for nearly anyone, *ad infinitum*. All in all, I suppose it simply re-proves the old computer-industry acronym GIGO (Garbage In, Garbage Out), and perhaps being hit by an asteroid is a preferable alternative to listening to such a plethora of commercial pap. But whatever you do, don't allow yourself to be distracted by the savage rantings of self-styled asinine audiophiles or ear-wax-impaired kit junkies. Just tap your foot to the strange rhythms in your head and listen to what you produce. Then decide what else, if anything, you might truly need.

Before you can get down to some serious recording, however, you'll need to be able to find your way around the various windows and controls in Cubase SX. The main windows provide access to various tools and key-control elements that will enable you to unlock the full power and functionality of Cubase SX. However, like driving a strange car or learning to fly an F-16, knowing where all the controls are and understanding exactly what they do can be a definite advantage.

the Transport panel

In Cubase SX, the Transport panel, like the familiar, traditional buttons found on analogue tape or video players, is used for controlling Record/Playback and other transport functions. With these controls you can play your recording, stop, wind forward or rewind just as you can on an analogue system. However, in Cubase SX, the Transport panel offers additional functionality and control over things like tempo and time signatures. It's also worth noting that the main transport functions - Play, Stop, Cycle and Record - are also available.

Left and right locator display, used to define where to start and end recording and which section to cycle

Position display

Tempo and time signature display

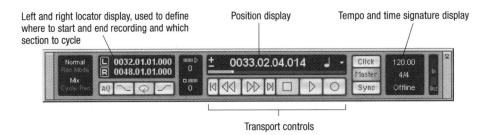

Transport controls

Position display

Nudge position right

Nudge position left

Position slider

Go to project start

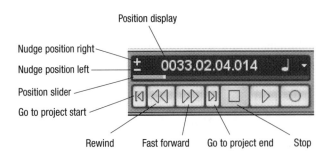

Rewind   Fast forward   Go to project end   Stop

At the far left of the Transport panel, you'll see the Record Mode selector. This determines whether Cubase SX will add any existing sound when recording takes place or overwrite what you've already recorded. The Record Mode selector affects only MIDI data and won't alter your audio recordings.

Immediately to the right of the Record Mode selector is a panel that contains settings for the left and right locators, the Cycle buttons, buttons for punching in and out of recordings and the AutoQuantize button. As you might guess, the top box indicates the current positions of the locators and defines where to start and end recording or what section to cycle. If you click on one of the locator labels (left or right), your song position is moved to the corresponding locator.

The Cycle button is used for cycling between the left and right locator positions. A cycle is essentially nothing more than a loop, the start and end points of which can be determined by setting the positions of the left and right locators. When the Cycle function is activated, you can listen to a section of your arrangement over and over again, recording more information each time.

If you've used a Portastudio or similar multitrack recorder or have done any work in a traditional studio you'll be familiar with a technique called *punching in*, or *dropping in*. This is the process of recording a new bit of a song onto a track while the tape is rolling. This function is particularly useful if you mess up a section of a vocal or lead line but the rest of the recording is actually OK. You simply run back the recording and drop in a replacement section over the flawed section and either punch out or carry on until the end. You can use either an automatic or a manual punch in.

TIP

If you've got a vocal or instrumental bit that is slightly off pitch and it's only a small section of an otherwise acceptable performance, don't drop or punch in a replacement. Instead, try using a pitch-correction plug-in to tweak and match the offending slips. With vocals, particularly, this maintains the feeling and organic flow of a piece, which can often be lost with a drop-in.

With the AutoQuantize button, you can choose to quantize everything you record, according to whatever quantizing type you've selected. As with practically everything in Cubase SX, if the result isn't what you expected or intended, it can easily be undone. (Incidentally, automatic quantizing applies only to MIDI recording and not to audio.)

Above these controls you'll find two timing-display bars, one showing the current song position in bars, beats and ticks and one a time-code readout showing the current song position in hours, minutes, seconds and frames.

At the far right, you'll find controls for activating the metronome, tempo and time-signature readouts and indicators that show MIDI-in (recording) and -out (playback) activity. There's also a Sync button for synchronising the sequencer to external devices. As you're probably aware, tempo determines the actual speed of your music and the number of beats per minute (usually quarter notes) and the time signature – ie 4/4, 3/4, etc – determines the overall feel of the beat and the grouping of notes. Perhaps the easiest way to set the tempo is to activate playback and adjust the tempo on the Transport panel while listening to the metronome pulse (triggered by the Click button) generated on each beat.

If necessary, you can change the size of the Transport panel and decide which parts of it you wish to be visible at any time. If you right-click anywhere within the Transport panel, a pop-up menu will appear from which you can check or uncheck elements of the Transport panel as desired.

the Project window

This is the main window in Cubase SX and provides you with an accessible graphic overview of your project, allowing you to navigate and get down to some hardcore editing. This is the magic circle (or, in this case, rectangle) in which you actually record and assemble your songs. Cubase was the first sequencer to implement the now-ubiquitous graphic Arrange window, allowing musical sections to be represented as rectangular blocks along a timeline. In Cubase SX, the Project window replaces the traditional Arrange window and song files have been superseded by project files, now identified with the .cpr extension.

Essentially, the Project window is divided vertically into tracks and has a timeline running horizontally from left to right. Each project has one Project window. Unlike previous versions of Cubase, such as VST, where you could have several Arrange windows, Cubase SX allows you to have only one Project window open at once. However, with SX you can have several projects open simultaneously, whereas with VST you could have only one song open at a time. It's also now possible for several projects to share the same Project folder. In SX, each audio track in the Project window is now automatically assigned to a unique audio channel, which unfortunately makes it impossible for multiple audio tracks to share the same channel, as they could before. Critics have complained that multiple takes of the same part now each require a separate audio channel when they're essentially part of the same track. However, in some respects, this new structure does force you to adopt a more organised way of working.

The new Project window does provide significantly more editing capabilities than previous versions of Cubase did, and it's now possible to edit with single-sample accuracy. Audio events can be displayed directly in the Project window, and all of the audio that you record or import into an SX project will always start off as an audio event. (In previous versions, the Arrange window could display only parts or collections of audio events, and it's still possible to make a collection of audio events into a part, which can be edited in the Audio Editor, as before. This can be particularly useful when you want to compile multiple vocal takes.) In SX, audio events are displayed with 'handles' that allow you to adjust the start and end points easily. You can also add fade-ins and -outs and adjust the overall level relative to the audio channel playing a particular audio event.

track types

In Cubase SX, you have the following track types are available in the Project window:

Audio
As you would imagine, you can use this track for recording and playing back audio events and parts. Each audio track has a corresponding audio channel in the Mixer, and an audio track can have any number of automation 'subtracks' for doing clever things like automating mixer-channel parameters and inserting effect settings.

Folder
As with folders on your PC, folder tracks here function as containers for other tracks, allowing you to edit several tracks at the same time, among other things.

Group Channels
Group channels function as subgroups and allow you to route several audio channels to a dedicated group channel. Afterwards, you can mix them with a single set of controls, allowing you to do things like apply the same effects to them. A group-channel track contains no events as such but displays settings and automation curves for the corresponding group channel. Each group-channel track has a corresponding channel strip in the Mixer.

MIDI Tracks
These are what you use for recording and playing back MIDI parts, and each MIDI track also has a corresponding MIDI channel strip in the Mixer. You can assign a MIDI track to have a number of automation 'subtracks' to enable the automating of parameters of Mixer channels, insert and send effect settings, etc.

Marker Track
The marker track displays...yes, you guessed it, markers, which can be moved and renamed directly in the Project window. However, there can be only one marker track in each project.

Master Automation

This control contains automation curves for master volume and global effect input levels, and, like the marker track, there can only be one Master Automation track in each project. However, you can expand the Master Automation control to display any number of automation curves.

Plug-In Automation

In Cubase SX, each send effect, master effect or VST instrument can have its own individual plug-in automation track, allowing for automation of all plug-in parameters. A plug-in automation track is automatically created the first time you automate any of a plug-in's parameters.

Video Tracks

I won't deal with these in any great detail, but as you can deduce, they're for playing back video events. If you do need to use this, remember that a project can have only one video track.

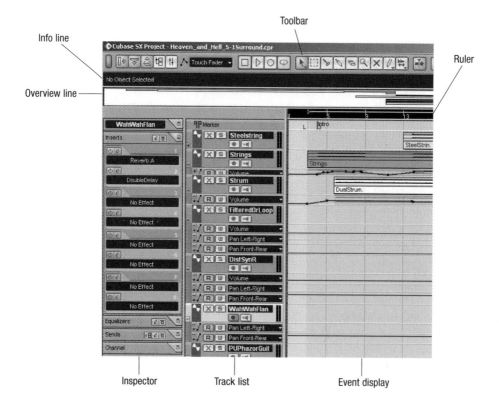

The Cubase SX Project window

parts and events

Think of events as Lego-like building blocks. When you build your project, you'll find that different event types are handled differently in the Project window, as follows:

- Video events and automation events (curve points) are always viewed and rearranged directly in the Project window.

- MIDI events are always gathered in MIDI parts, while containers for one or more MIDI events and MIDI parts are rearranged and manipulated in the Project window. To edit the individual MIDI events in a part, you have to open the part in a MIDI editor.

- Audio events can be displayed and edited directly in the Project window, but you can also work with audio parts containing several events. This is particularly useful if you have a number of events that you want to treat as one unit in the project.

An audio event (left) and an audio part (right)

the Track list

On the left in the Project window you'll find the Track list, which contains name fields and various settings for each track. Different track types have different controls in the Track list. Depending on your display size, to see all of the controls you might have to experiment with resizing the required track in the Track list.

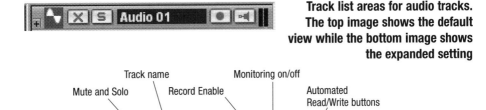

Track list areas for audio tracks. The top image shows the default view while the bottom image shows the expanded setting

Track name

Mute and Solo

Record Enable

Monitoring on/off

Automated Read/Write buttons

Output activity indicator

Indicates whether effect sends, EQ or insert effects are activated for the track. Click to bypass

Stereo on/off

Musical linear time base

Lock track

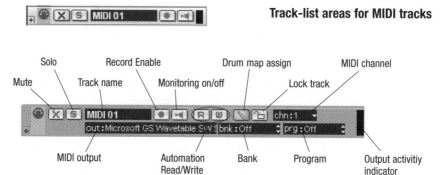

Track-list areas for MIDI tracks

the Inspector

Moving unfashionably further to the left, you'll find an area called the Inspector. This can show additional controls and parameters for the track selected in the Track list, and if several tracks are selected, the Inspector shows the setting for the first (topmost) selected track. To hide or show the Inspector, click the Inspector icon in the toolbar.

The contents and usage of the Inspector depends on the selected track's class. For some classes of track, the Inspector is divided into sections. You can hide or show sections by clicking the tabs in their top-right-hand corners. Clicking the tab for a hidden section brings it into view and hides the other sections, while [Ctrl]-clicking the tab allows you to hide or show a section without affecting other sections. Finally, Alt-clicking a tab shows or hides all sections in the Inspector. (It should be noted that folding a section does not affect the functionality but merely hides the section from view. In other words, if you've set up a track parameter or activated an effect, your settings will still be active even if you fold the Inspector section.)

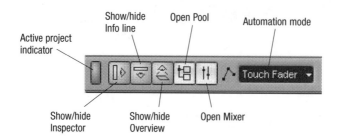

The Cubase SX inspector

the Toolbar

As in recent versions of Cubase, in SX, various tools used in different situations are gathered in toolboxes or toolbars. Most windows in Cubase SX have their own particular toolbar, each with appropriate variations. Essentially, the toolbar contains tools and shortcuts for opening other windows and various project settings and functions.

In some respects, the toolbox familiar in earlier versions of Cubase has been superseded in SX. The Quick menu is displayed as a normal Windows pop-up menu, although it still provides a selection of tools to which users have become accustomed. In SX, the Quick menu also provides a list of context-sensitive options based on whichever elements you've currently selected onscreen and the position of the mouse when you clicked to access the menu.

The toolbox is now also displayed along the toolbar of every window, providing a second method of accessing whatever you need for editing. SX will now let you select tools via the number keys on the main PC keyboard – not, as you might think, from the numeric keypad. Logically, the keys that select the various tools – number keys 1-8 – follow the same running order as the tools that normally appear in the Project window. However, in a most un-Spock-like illogical manner, in other editors where the order of the tools differs, the number keys still dumbly follow the order in the Project window.

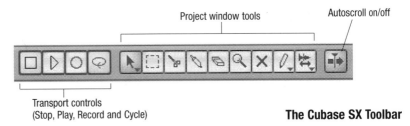

Project window tools   Autoscroll on/off

Transport controls
(Stop, Play, Record and Cycle)

The Cubase SX Toolbar

the Info line

The Info line shows information about whichever event or part has been selected in the Project window. You can edit almost all values in the Info line by using regular value editing. Length and position values are displayed in the format currently selected for the ruler, and the Info line can be hidden or revealed by clicking the corresponding icon on the toolbar. The following elements can also be selected for display and editing on the Info line:

•   Audio events
•   Audio parts

- MIDI parts
- Video events
- Markers
- Automation-curve points

It's worth noting that the Info line will display information only if a single element is selected.

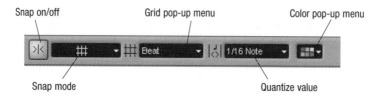

Snap on/off   Grid pop-up menu   Color pop-up menu

Snap mode   Quantize value

The Cubase SX Info line

the Ruler

This is found at the top of the Event display and shows the Timeline. Initially, the Ruler in the Project window uses the display format specified in the Project Setup dialog box, just like all of the other rulers and position displays in the project. However, you can select an independent display format for the Ruler by clicking on the arrow button to the right of it and selecting an option from the pop-up menu that appears. The selection you make here affects the Ruler, the Info line and tool-tip position values appearing when you drag an event in the Project window. You can also select independent formats for other rulers and position displays. To set the display format globally for all windows, use the Display Format pop-up menu on the Transport panel or hold down [Ctrl] and select a display format in any ruler.

The Project window Ruler

sequencers – short back and sides

Back in the old days, sequencers handled only MIDI; they weren't capable of handling audio until some years later, when PCs and hard drives got faster and cheaper. Modern digital sequencers are generally capable of providing an impressive number of audio and MIDI tracks, depending on the processing power of your PC, the speed of your hard disk and the interface you use to get things in and out and connect external devices. As you've probably gathered by now, Cubase SX is a fully integrated state-of-the-art software sequencer suitable for recording, editing and processing both MIDI and audio, literally the magic ingredient that turns your PC into a virtual recording studio. Sophisticated consistency of design ensures that Cubase SX on the PC and on the Mac provides a very intuitive and direct interface featuring a comprehensive set of new menus, keyboard shortcuts, pop-up menus, drag-and-drop editing and a whole raft of features that will already be familiar to seasoned users. But, like any powerful application, it does take some getting used to, and actually getting the sort of sound and recording quality that you require might take a bit of practice, patience and an element of experimentation, so don't be afraid to try things out. Generally, anything you do can be undone, and rarely will a healthy heuristic approach to creativity result in anything disastrous. Just as the best music often comes out of improvised jams, the best recordings are often made when you bend the rules or ignore them completely and just work on creative intuition. Getting your head around how a sequencer like Cubase SX works isn't really much more difficult than figuring out how to use a four- or eight-track Portastudio. (Well, maybe a little.) And you'll definitely find that you have a lot more freedom, control and functionality with a digital studio than you would with even some of the best analogue equipment. For example, things like room acoustics and background noise become less of an issue when recording in a digital environment because you can edit and clean up your signal and add effects to simulate any kind of room or ambience you desire.

Cubase SX is one of those applications that can stretch as far as you want to stretch it. As I said in the introduction, this book is designed particularly for musicians and producers who simply want to have a go at creating music with a digital studio. Sure, hardcore tech-heads or even sound engineers and technicians with loads of traditional studio experience will be able to use Cubase SX and explain everything you never wanted to know about decibels, waveforms, impedance, ohms, room acoustics and the like, and it's cool and extremely impressive that an application like Cubase SX can offer so much to so many different users. But don't be overawed by all the science and, above all, don't let it get in the way of the music. As long as you've got a reasonably good microphone, some basic MIDI kit and perhaps some sort of sampling capability, you can easily produce music that will sound as good, if not better, than most of the stuff currently being produced commercially. OK, maybe that's not all that hard and should probably be discouraged at all costs. However, if you want to know all the related science and techie bits, there are plenty of books out there to choose from. If you just want to play, compose and record interesting music, then learn how to do what you need for what you want to produce, even if you don't fully comprehend all the jargon and technical explanations behind it.

Science or no science, though, before you get down to some serious recording, you do have to have some idea of how to get an audio signal into your PC, how to record and manipulate MIDI data and how you're then going to produce it in a form that you can feed back into the real world.

what is digital audio?

Audio, or just plain sound, comes from any source that you can connect to a sound input on your PC. With the right bits and pieces, you can use a microphone, keyboard, electric guitar - essentially, anything with a plug. Raw audio input becomes digital audio when your PC and add-on soundcard converts the signal into numbers (via an analogue-to-digital converter) which Cubase SX then captures and stores on your hard drive. Once your digital audio is in the box, you can creatively start to manipulate and process your recordings. As I mentioned earlier, it's absolutely vital to remember that audio files tend to be exceedingly large when they're written to your hard disk during the actual recording process. This is why storage size is important when it comes to planning your system, and also why you should always defragment your drive before starting a recording session.

The quality of your digital audio data depends entirely on the performance of the converters found in your audio card, as well as the data's sampling rate and bit resolution. When people talk about a sampling rate, all they mean is the number of times an analogue signal is measured each second, while bit resolution - usually found in measures of 8, 16, 20 and 24 - describes the accuracy of the system measuring the signal. The higher the number of bits, the more levels of resolution are available to measure the analogue signal. Assuming that your PC is meaty enough, each project in Cubase SX will support a maximum of 200 audio and 64 group tracks, with 96kHz sampling rates and up to 32-bit resolution. While every audio file in a project must use the same sample rate in Cubase SX, it's still possible to mix and match bit depths, if necessary. This can be particularly useful if you want to, say, bounce 16-bit audio tracks and keep the internal 32-bit resolution used by most insert effects.

Considering that bog-standard audio CDs handle only 16 bits, this high degree of resolution might seem like overkill, but in reality the situation is sort of analogous to graphics scanning: images are typically scanned at very high resolutions - up to 2,400 dots per square inch - even though no printing device on Earth can cope with such dense grids of ink. (Colour images are normally printed at a maximum of 200dpi, while greyscale ones seldom exceed 300dpi.) The reason for this is that the graphics expert gets far better results by scanning an image at these enormously high resolutions and then, when the image is ready for printing, 'dithering' down to a grid more acceptable to image setters and high-resolution laser printers. All the data is present in the original file and can be reprocessed, if necessary. Audio can be treated in exactly the same way, although in the end all CD-based audio must be reduced to 16 bits, as far greater initial accuracy can be obtained by scanning (ie recording) at these very high resolutions and then mastering at 16 bits.

If you've worked with Portastudios or other analogue multitrack recorders, you should understand that there are some aspects of working with digital audio that require a different approach. In traditional studios, it's not unusual to push certain sound signals so that VU meters occasionally peak into the red. In an analogue environment, this sort of technique can add a natural kind of warmth to a mix, and although it produces mild, graduated distortion, this tends to be rounded off and is hardly ever offensive to the ear. With digital audio, however, you can't allow levels to go into the red without getting a truly nasty distortion known as *clipping*. With Cubase SX, you must therefore ensure that no clipping occurs, and you might find that you need to record at analogue sources lower average levels than you're used to.

However, as I suggested earlier, you'll find that the advantages offered by digital audio generally outweigh the occasional disadvantages. Apart from the convenience of storing it on your hard disk, digital audio tends to have less background noise and hiss, provides a better dynamic range and can be copied with no loss of quality. And with Cubase SX and an assortment of VST plug-ins, you can easily apply a whole range of signal-processing effects.

what is MIDI?

MIDI is another one of those annoying acronyms and stands for Musical Instrument Digital Interface. It's essentially a form of computer code that was developed as a means by which synths and other devices could be connected up so that they could talk to and interact with one another. For any techies that may have tuned in, MIDI is an asynchronous, serial interface transmitted at the rate of 31.25kbaud, or 31,250 bits per second. For the rest of us, a MIDI synthesiser or similar device works a bit like a musical printer – your PC sends information to it specifying the notes, sound, instrument type etc that you want to play and it gets on with creating the actual audio. This means that you can take a recording made on, say, a piano and play it back on a guitar sound just by changing the settings on your synth.

General MIDI, or GM as it's usually referred to, was an attempt to create a standard system for MIDI parameters whereby songs created on one GM-compatible synth could be played back on any other GM synth and sound something like the original. In other words, if an original composition specifies particular sounds to be played, then when any other GM synth is handed the GM MIDI file to play it will reproduce the correct sounds assigned by the original composer. In practice, for particularly mundane applications such as playing and singing along to a sequenced backing of 'Wild Rover' down the pub, this sort of system works fine – landlord buys a GM MIDI file of 'Wild Rover', punter loads it up in a drunken stupor, hits Play and all of the sounds that should be heard will play back. Everyone sings badly and bangs the table at the appropriate time, spilling puddles of beer all over the floor.

However, GM does have two main restrictions. One is that you're tied to a fairly standard, unadventurous palette of sounds, so if you've created some wicked tune featuring a clever little sound that you've programmed on some non-GM device, this sound won't be recognised by GM and could come out sounding like a duck.

The other restriction involves controllers. Since GM specifies fixed controller numbers for certain functions, while basic parameters such as pan, volume and sustain are represented, unfortunately more advanced functions such as filter resonance and cut-off time are not.

GM was agreed as a standard in 1991 by the JMSC (Japanese MIDI Standards Committee) and the MMA (American MIDI Manufacturers' Association). General MIDI System Level 1 specifies 24-note polyphonic, 16-part multitimbral operation; all of the drum sounds are defined by note number and the 128 sound patches for the other instruments are also defined.

GS and XG

There are also extensions of the GM standard called GS and XG. GS is Roland's extended version of GM which adds some extras on top of the GM settings by utilising the GM Bank Select command. MIDI has a fixed range of 0-127 for all parameters (although some manufacturers use 1-128), so original GM allows for only 128 sound patches, all stored in one bank, while the GM Bank Select command allows for further banks to be accessed, each with a further 128 patches. Also added are extra NRPNs (Non-Registered Parameter Numbers), which provide extra controller numbers, allowing you to twiddle things like filter control and envelope control and giving you extra effects parameters. In practice, GS files will play back on a GM synth, but none of the extras will be recognised by anything other than another GS-compatible device.

As with the Roland GS standard, XG is Yamaha's own dedicated version, also offering extra sounds and control parameters. However, these are not recognisable by GM or Roland, and vice versa.

GETTING STARTED

parts and events

When you're recording MIDI or entering MIDI data manually in an editor, you're creating *MIDI events*. Each note you record is a separate MIDI event, for example, and if you record the movement of a modulation wheel or other controller, a large number of densely spaced MIDI events are created. MIDI events are always grouped in *MIDI parts*, which can be thought of as containers, allowing you to move or copy a number of MIDI events as one item. These MIDI parts are placed on MIDI tracks, and for each MIDI track you can specify on which MIDI output and MIDI channel its MIDI events should be played back. This allows you to have different tracks playing back different sounds on the same or different MIDI instruments.

OK, while MIDI can seem a bit confusing and, indeed, downright cantankerous to wire up properly, it's extremely useful when it comes to digital recording. However, you'll be pleased to know that Cubase SX supports not only General MIDI but also both extensions from Roland and Yamaha.

35

audio and MIDI

The way in which you configure your system for Cubase SX will ultimately depend on what kind of music you intend to make, what kind of external devices you require and how elaborate you want to make your personal recording environment. Obviously, for making even the simplest MIDI-based recordings, you'll need some sort of input device such as a synth, a MIDI keyboard and, perhaps, a sampler, while for audio recordings the minimum is probably a microphone of some description that will plug into the audio input of your PC or audio card or perhaps an electric guitar or bass. You might want to start with a small-scale system that provides the minimum set-up necessary to record and play MIDI and audio in Cubase and then work up to a larger set-up, or you might want to customise your own personalised system to look something like the digital-studio layouts suggested in the illustrations here. The audio connections below can be either digital or analogue, it doesn't really matter.

setting up audio
stereo input and output – the simplest connection

If you use only a stereo input and output from Cubase SX, you might connect your audio hardware directly to the input source - a mixer, for example - and the outputs to a power amplifier and speaker. When connecting an input source - a mixer, say - to your audio hardware, you should use an output bus or similar that's separate from the mixer's master output in order to avoid recording what you're playing back.

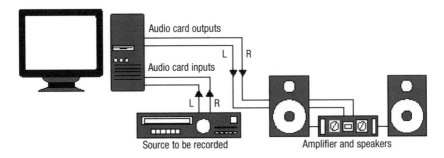

Audio card outputs
L R
Audio card inputs
L R
Source to be recorded
Amplifier and speakers

Stereo input/output set-up

multichannel input and output

More often than not, you'll have other audio equipment that you want to integrate with Cubase SX. This will require a mixer, preferably one with a group or bus system that can be used for feeding inputs on the audio hardware. For example, you could use four buses for feeding signals to the sound hardware's inputs. Four outputs would be connected back to the mixer for monitoring and playback purposes and the remaining mixer inputs could then be used for connecting audio sources such as microphones, instruments and samplers.

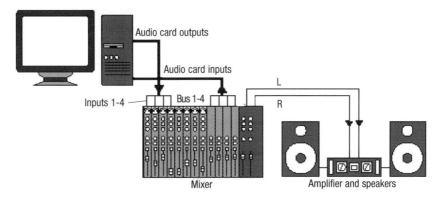

Multi-channel input/output set-up

connecting for surround sound

If you plan to mix for surround sound, you could connect the audio outputs of your devices to a multichannel power amplifier driving a set of surround channels. For example, the connection shown below will work for mixing both 5.1 and LRCS (eg Pro Logic) where, say, two surround speakers will be playing the same material from a single surround channel. The only difference between the two formats here is the LFE channel, which isn't used with LRCS. Fortunately, Cubase SX supports a number of surround formats.

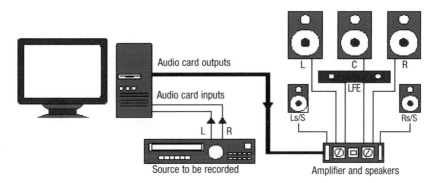

Surround-sound set-up

recording from a CD player

Most computers come with a CD-ROM drive that can also be used as a regular CD player. Normally, the CD player is connected internally to the audio hardware so that you can record its output directly into Cubase SX. All routing and level adjustments are then done in the audio-hardware set-up application, shown in the illustration over the page. You can also grab audio tracks directly from a CD in Cubase SX.

Word Clock connections

If you're using a digital audio connection, you might also need a Word Clock connection between the audio hardware and any external devices you're using. Don't forget that it's very important that you synchronise with the Word Clock correctly or you could end up with a lot of crackles and clicks on some of your recordings.

audio hardware set-up

You'll often find that audio hardware has several inputs – say, for a microphone input, line inputs, assorted digital inputs and usually a connection from the CD-ROM drive in your PC. With audio hardware, you should receive one or more small applications that allow you to configure the inputs of the hardware to your own particular tastes. These sort of functions include:

• Selecting which in/outs are active

• Setting up Word Clock synchronisation (if available)

• Turning monitoring via hardware on/off

• Setting levels for each input

• Setting levels for the outputs so that they match the monitoring equipment you're using

For more details about your audio-hardware set-up application, always refer to the documentation that came with the hardware. Yes, it is boring, but it's still important.

As I mentioned earlier on, Steinberg strongly recommend that you access your hardware via an ASIO driver written specifically for the hardware you're using, if available. If no ASIO driver is installed, they suggest that you check with the manufacturer of your audio hardware to see if they have an ASIO driver available – for download via the internet, for example. If your hardware doesn't have a specific ASIO driver, Steinberg state that a DirectX driver is the next best option.

To set up your own system, select 'Device Setup' from the Devices menu and click on 'VST Multitrack' in the list that pops up. Select your particular audio hardware from the ASIO Driver menu.

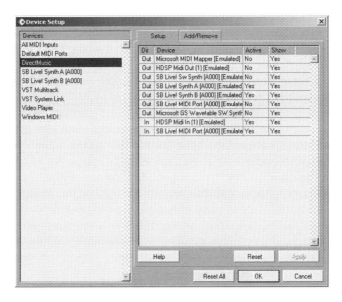

Device set-up menu

Click the Control Panel button and adjust the settings as recommended by your audio hardware's manufacturer. Remember, the control panel that appears when you click on this button will be provided by the audio hardware manufacturer and not Cubase SX (unless you're using DirectX or MME), so settings will be different for each brand and model of audio card and may include options for such criteria as buffering, synchronisation and digital-input and -output formats. If you're planning to use several different audio applications simultaneously, you might want to activate the option 'Release ASIO Driver In Background', which will allow another application to play back via your audio hardware even when Cubase SX is running. In this instance, the application that is currently active, or sitting in the top window on the desktop, will get access to the audio hardware. Just make sure that any other audio applications accessing the audio hardware are also set to release the ASIO driver so that Cubase can use it when it becomes the active application again. (Incidentally, if your audio hardware and its driver support ASIO Direct Monitoring, you might want to activate the 'Direct Monitoring' checkbox.) When you've finished, click 'Apply' and then 'OK' to close the dialog box.

setting up MIDI

Below is an example of a fairly typical small MIDI set-up. You might need or want to hook things up differently, of course, and in this example I've assumed that you have some sort of MIDI keyboard and an external MIDI sound module. The keyboard can be used for feeding MIDI messages to your PC to activate the recording and playback of MIDI tracks, while the sound module is used for playback only. By using Cubase SX's MIDI Thru feature, you'll be able to hear the correct sound from the sound module while you're actually playing the keyboard or recording.

Of course, you might want to use even more instruments for playback, and if so, simply connect the MIDI Thru socket on the sound module to MIDI In of the next instrument, and so on. In this hook-up, you'll always play the first keyboard when recording, but you can still use all of your devices for providing sounds on playback. If you plan to use more than three sound sources, Steinberg recommend that you use either an interface with more than one output or a separate MIDI Thru box instead of the Thru jacks on each unit.

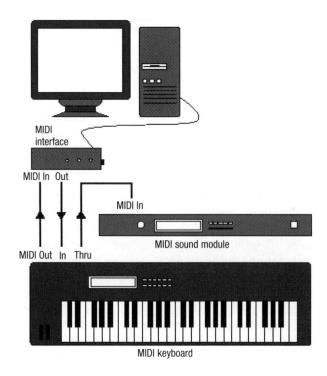

Typical MIDI set-up

setting up a default MIDI input and output

You might want to make sure that any new tracks you create are set to particular MIDI ports, and fortunately this is fairly easy to do. To begin with, select 'Device Setup' from the Devices menu and click on 'Default MIDI Ports' in the list that appears. Make sure that the Setup tab is selected and then use the two pop-ups to select an input and an output. Now, newly created tracks will always use this input and output. (Don't worry – like most things in SX, you can change this setting for each individual track in the Project window at any time.) To finish off, click 'Apply' and then 'OK' to close the dialog box.

TIP

You'll notice in Cubase SX that MIDI inputs and outputs can often be shown with unnecessarily long and complex names. However, if you like, you can rename your MIDI ports with shorter, sexier and more descriptive names. Simply open the 'Device Setup' dialog box from the Devices menu and select the Windows MIDI device in the Device list. The available MIDI inputs and outputs are all listed under the Setup tab. To change the name of a MIDI port, click in the Device column and type in a new name of the port. After closing the dialog box, the new name will appear on the MIDI In and Out windows, as well as in the pop-ups in the Inspector and Track Mixer.

setting MIDI Thru and Local On/Off

To do this, first go to the File menu and open the Preferences dialog. In the MIDI section, you'll find a setting called 'MIDI Thru Active' which can be switched on or off. Its status is related to a setting in your instrument called 'Local On/Off' or 'Local Control On/Off'. MIDI Thru should be activated and instruments should be set to 'Local Off', or 'Local Control Off'. The MIDI signal from the keyboard will then be recorded into Cubase SX and at the same time rerouted back to the instrument so that you can hear what you're playing without the keyboard triggering its own sounds.

If you're using a separate MIDI keyboard that doesn't produce any of its own sounds, MIDI Thru in Cubase SX should also be activated. This time you don't have to look for any Local On/Off settings in your instruments; the only occasion when MIDI Thru should be *deactivated* is when you're using Cubase SX with only one keyboard instrument and when that instrument can't be set to Local Off mode. You should also remember that MIDI Thru will only be active for MIDI tracks that are record enabled.

When MIDI Thru is active in Cubase SX, MIDI data received is immediately 'echoed' back out so that, when you press a key, it's sent out via MIDI to Cubase. Any MIDI data coming in to the instrument is then played by the synth inside it, so when Local (Control) is set to 'On' on the instrument, the keys you press will be played by the internal synth. When Local (Control) is set to Off, this connection is broken.

TIP

If you want to use remote-control devices, such as Steinberg's Houston, in conjunction with Cubase SX, it's important to observe that remote-control data is recorded to MIDI tracks and 'thrued' when the track input is set to 'All MIDI Inputs'. In some cases, not only the track mixer but also MIDI instruments routed to that track will be unintentionally remote-controlled. In order to avoid this, you should exclude single MIDI In ports from the 'All MIDI Input' setting. To do this, go to the Devices menu and open 'Device Setup'. There, in the category 'All MIDI Inputs', you'll see that single MIDI In ports can be deactivated. From here, every port that is accessed by a remote-control device should be deactivated.

working practices

Once you understand the basics of how Cubase SX works, the best way to master it is to get in there and start experimenting. Trial and error is an excellent teacher, and finding things out for yourself is always more valuable then being spoonfed someone else's opinions every step of the way. After all, that's the only way you'll ever develop your own unique approach and creative method. But before we look at some actual studio and recording tips, let's look at some of the other peripheral equipment you'll need to get the best results from Cubase SX and your own performance.

Once your PC, MIDI and Cubase connections are sorted out, there are a few additional priorities that you really can't afford to neglect if you're interested in making serious recordings. Firstly, if your budget's tight and you have to cut corners, whatever you do, *don't* skimp on your microphones. This is one bit of advice that cannot be over-emphasised. I mean, think about it – despite all the clever digital trickery, it's still difficult to make the final sound you ultimately produce better than the original source signal. If your budget is limited, buy one or two high-quality mics rather than several low-quality ones. As a matter of fact, to begin with, if money is tight, buy only one exceptionally good mic; you can do more with one good mic than any number of substandard models, even though in some instances it might seem like having several cheaper ones would make sessions more convenient. However, if you can have only one mic, try to have something like an AKG C-414. There's practically no sound that these mics don't do at least a good job with, and they usually retail at slightly under £500 ($800), although you might find them cheaper if you shop around. If that's still out of your price range, the AKG C-3000 or the Audio Technica 4033 are both pretty decent mics which sell for under

£300 ($470). There are also a number of other modestly priced condenser mics coming onto the market that would also be worth a look. If you're on a really tight budget, the Shure SM57 and SM58 are good performing workhorses that can also be used for reasonable recording. But if you can't come up with that...well, how serious are you?

effects and processors

With the wide range of VST plug-ins available today, you don't need a massive rack full of signal processors – reverbs, delays, etc – to make a pro-quality recording; that sort of stuff always looks impressive, but when you come right down to it, it's not essential. If you can afford them, one or two good reverbs and a couple of good-quality compressors could be useful, and there are several decent low-priced reverbs currently on the market, including the Alesis Quadraverb, the Lexicon LXP-1 and the Yamaha REV-500. You can also find acceptable low-priced compressors like the DBX 160A and the RNC at reasonable prices, and it's always worth trying to pick up second-hand units as well.

While there are advantages to some of these hardware processors, you should definitely check out the range of VST plug-ins that offer digital equivalents of all of these sorts of effects. OK, none of the hardware units I've mentioned is going to startle the world or give you a Top Ten hit, but if they're used correctly and creatively they can yield surprisingly professional results without sending you to the bank for a second mortgage.

media matters

Since the chances are you'll be recording directly to your hard drive, you won't have to worry too much about things like ADATs or multitrack tape. However, a DAT or MiniDisc recorder can be useful for dubbing down master mixes or for mastering and pressing CDs. While the MiniDisc format is a good, cheap digital medium, do keep in mind that it does perform some very funky data compression and, depending on how you use it, this can occasionally wreck the harmonics and overtones in your material.

other hardware

If you're at all serious about production, at some point you're going to need an external mixing desk. A good one to start with is the 16-channel Mackie or perhaps the Spirit 12-channel Folio. There are always a new, improved and cheaper mixers coming onto the market, but as with everything else it's worth shopping around and checking out second-hand sources as well.

If you can afford it, it might also be a good idea to pick up a good-quality microphone pre-amp. This is not to say that the pre-amps in all mixers are particularly bad – the ones in the Mackie, for example, are pretty good – but even many mid- to upper-mid-level mixing desks can have mediocre mic pre-amps. The only reason for this that I can think of is that most pro engineers have their own outboard mic pre-amps that they like to work with and probably don't use the ones in their consoles, so the manufacturers figure that it's pointless jacking up the pre-amps and the price when nobody is going to care anyway. Good low-priced pre-amps to look for are Symetrix and DBX models, although they might not be a great improvement on the ones in most desks. Really good mic pre-amps cost at least as much as top-notch mics, and if you've got the cash (or the credit) you're better off springing for an Avalon or Focusrite model. However, be warned: once you use one, you'll never be happy with anything less.

Monitor speakers will also have a great impact on the finished sound of your mixes, so don't use those three-ways that came with your JVC stereo system. In the affordable range, you could consider models like the JBL and the industry-standard Yamaha NS-10, neither of which sound all that incredible and yet seem to mix very well once you're used to them. The problem with monitoring your material over your home stereo is that consumer speakers have built-in EQ curves and other devices designed to sweeten the sound that they produce. What you want to hear from a mix when you're monitoring, however, is the absolute sonic truth. Pro audio monitors don't lie (well, at least not nearly as much), and it's also worth keeping a pair of really cheap boombox speakers nearby just to reference things once in a while. After you've been mixing for a few hours, your ears tend to go woolly, and you'd be surprised how a mix can sound like the voice of God over good speakers and later like muddy trash over your friend's Audiovox car system. It therefore pays to have at least two sets of monitors: a set of good ones and a set of fairly crap ones.

session planning

Without going into a lot of detail about how to plan your recording session, it's worth mentioning a few basic practices that you might already be familiar with. The way in which you actually structure your recording session will, of course, depend on the generic style of the music you want to create and the instrumentation and arrangements involved. However, in most instances, it's best to start by laying down rhythm and bass tracks, either to a click track or a guide vocal, or possibly to a main MIDI track. Once you've got the rhythm, bass and chord parts down, you've effectively established the structure and shape of the song and you can build, layer and arrange from there. The nice thing about Cubase SX is that it makes it easy for you to adjust the mix as you record new parts so that, by the time you've got everything recorded, you've got a mix that will be pretty close to your desired final sound.

Also, while this may be restating the obvious, it's absolutely imperative that you tune all of your instruments with a tuner before you start any recording session. Despite what a lot of musicians may claim, most of us don't have perfect or even relative pitch, and a properly tuned instrument is one of the first key elements you need to get right in order to make a good recording. It also means that you won't run into problems later when you start laying down a track with a new instrument only to discover that somewhere in the previous mix of tracks there's an out-of-tune guitar. (Incidentally, most MIDI instruments are tuneable as well, so make sure that all of your instruments are at least in tune with each other – it will make your life a lot easier.)

The way in which you organise your sessions depends entirely on the line-up of instruments at your disposal, as well as the type of music and the generic sound you're trying to create. Once you get into recording sessions, you'll discover that there are several different ways of doing the same job and that most people will simply choose the one they like best and use it most of the time.

chapter 4

studio session 1: laying down tracks

C reating and playing music should be fun, so there's no reason why recording and mixing it shouldn't be fun as well. As you've probably gathered by now, your PC and Cubase SX provide the equivalent of a hugely powerful studio system at a fraction of the cost of a traditional tape-based recording set-up. And, as an added bonus, you can even set it up and record in the comfort of your own home. So, unlike so many other things in life, Cubase SX offers a wonderful and convenient opportunity to be creative, make music and have fun, all at the same time.

logistics

For most serious recording, you'll definitely need an external mixer, and since the mixing desk has always been the centre of a traditional recording studio, you'll want to keep your mixer close to your PC system so that you can operate both without moving from your ideal monitoring position. MIDI keyboards and samplers can be positioned to one side or even underneath your keyboard position, and you can experiment with racking or tiered arrangements. Just remember that nothing should be placed or racked higher than the bottom of your monitor speakers or anywhere between the monitors and your head. Make sure your cables are kept out of harm's way and avoid running mains leads alongside signal cables or you'll pick up ground-loop hum. Don't ever remove any earth leads from any equipment, and if you're using multiplug extension blocks, once you've plugged everything in, make sure you leave it plugged in, as plugging and unplugging your gear will weaken contacts and you could end up with dodgy connections creating annoying pops and crackles.

If you usually work alone, try to get hold of a combined mic, pre-amp and compressor for your audio recording, as these work reasonably well for recording vocals or instruments. Also, make sure you've got a reasonably long mic lead, since you'll want to get your mic as far away from your computer and peripherals as possible in order to avoid picking up hum and fan noise.

While real voices and miked instruments are affected by the acoustic environment in which they're recorded, you can do quite a lot with Cubase SX to enhance, process and fix that sound, so don't panic if you don't have total isolation facilities or you get a bit of bleed-through or background noise. One of the disadvantages of the digital revolution in music has been a sort of compulsive obsession with perfectly pure audio hygiene. Personally, I think that a completely clean sound is over-rated, rather sterile and generally totally inoffensive to the average ear (unless you're an anally retentive audio geek). After all, the natural world is full of interference and unintended reverberation, and rarely – particularly in a live performance – is music heard in the acoustic equivalent of a hermetically sealed environment. Let's face it, some genres of music actually benefit from a lo-fi approach, and despite what you might hear from the cultural prudes, a bit of audio dirt can, in many instances, add an important element of warmth and soul.

TIP

When you record, always record dry (ie with no effects), as effects like reverb and VST plug-ins are extremely heavy on processing power. It's therefore always advisable to add effects after you've laid down your tracks. A general tip for both music production and for Cubase in general is to remember always that less is more and that, just because you have the functionality, you don't need to use it. And when it comes to arrangements and mixes, don't use six violins if you can use two - use only what you need when you need it. Remember, depending on the style of music you play and the way you want your final recording to sound, there may be whole sections of Cubase SX that you'll never bother to use. Don't worry about it. If you can produce a recording that accurately reflects the sound you want to hear, you're probably using everything you need.

fundamentals of recording

In many respects, Cubase SX is as easy to use as a simple analogue tape recorder, with the added bonus that you can record on a single track or on several audio and/or MIDI tracks simultaneously. To begin recording on a track, all you need to do is make one ready for recording by clicking its Record Enable button in the Track list, found in either the Inspector or the Mixer. When activated, the button will turn red, letting you know that you're ready to record. Exactly how many audio tracks (for example) you can record simultaneously will depend on the performance of your CPU and hard disk, although it's always worth remembering that there's no point in recording more audio tracks than you have audio inputs, since this would only result in unnecessary duplicate tracks and audio files.

**Record button enabled on Inspector (left),
Mixer (centre) and Track list (right)**

To begin recording, click the Record button on the Transport panel or toolbar, or use the corresponding key command (default [*]) on the numeric keypad. You can activate recording while you're in Stop mode (from the current cursor position or from the left locator) or during playback. If you activate recording from Stop mode and the option 'Start Record At Left Locator' is selected on the Transport panel, recording will unsurprisingly start from the left locator. If you activate recording from Stop mode and the 'Start Record At Left Locator' is deactivated, recording will start from the cursor's position in the current project. However, if you activate recording during playback, Cubase SX will immediately enter Record mode and start recording at the current project's cursor position. As I mentioned earlier, this procedure is known as a *manual punch-in* and is particularly useful if you need to replace a section of a recording and want to listen to the previously recorded audio up to the recording's start position. All you need to do is set the left locator to the position where you want to start recording, activate the Punch In button on the Transport panel and then activate playback from some position before the left locator. When the Project cursor reaches the left locator, recording will start automatically.

Punch In and Punch Out buttons activated

You can also stop your recording either automatically or manually. If you click the Stop button on the Transport panel or use the keyboard shortcut (default [0] on the numeric keypad), recording is deactivated and Cubase SX goes back to Stop mode. If you click the Record button or use the key command for recording (default [*]), recording will be deactivated but playback will continue. This is the *manual punch-out* described earlier. If the Punch Out button is activated on the Transport panel, recording will be deactivated when the Project cursor reaches the right locator, executing an automatic punch-out.

As discussed in Chapter 2, with Cubase SX you can also record and play back a loop by using the Cycle function. To create a loop, simply specify the start and end points by setting the left and right locators in the desired positions. When the Cycle button is engaged, by clicking the Cycle button on the Transport panel, the selected section will repeat seamlessly *ad infinitum* until you hit Stop or deactivate Cycle mode. To record in Cycle mode, you can start recording from the left locator, from before the locators or from within the loop itself, either from Stop mode or during playback. As soon as the Project cursor reaches the right locator, it will jump back to the left locator and continue recording a new lap. When using Cycle mode, however, keep in mind that the overall results of cycle-recording audio and MIDI are always somewhat different. And remember that, if you decide that you don't like what you've just recorded, you can always delete it by selecting Undo from the Edit menu.

The Transport panel showing the Cycle button engaged

OK, that's the fundamentals out of the way. As I mentioned in Chapter 2, all of your recording, editing and arranging for both audio and MIDI will be done within the Project window. Now let's have a look at how to go about laying down some MIDI and audio tracks.

recording MIDI

As I mentioned earlier, in Cubase SX there's less of a distinction between the way in which MIDI and audio are handled in the recording process than perhaps there was in previous versions. This is generally seen as a good thing, although

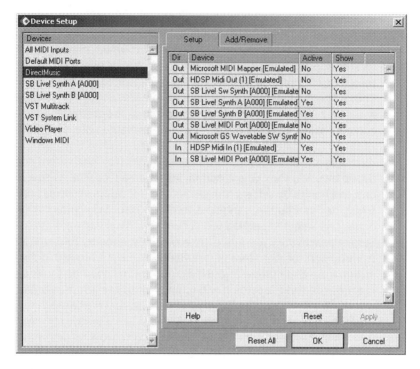

**Before recording, make sure you've sorted all of your
MIDI settings in the Device Setup menu**

there have been a few grumbles about the loss of a few working features. Traditionally, a lot of musicians find recording MIDI a bit easier than recording audio, since with a MIDI keyboard, for example, you can essentially record all of the various parts of your musical composition one at a time and then play them back together in perfect synchronisation. As with most things in the digital studio, all of your sounds, tempi, effects etc can of course still be chopped, changed and altered *ad infinitum*.

Before you begin your MIDI recording session, you'd be wise to double-check the following:

• Is your MIDI interface connected and working properly?

• Have you connected a MIDI keyboard or other controller and a MIDI sound source?

• Is your sound source General MIDI, GS or XG compatible?

Incidentally, if your keyboard or sound source isn't GM compatible, you won't be able to select sounds from the pop-up menus in Cubase SX. To do this, make sure that your MIDI keyboard is connected to the MIDI In of your MIDI interface.

If you're doing some serious production, I'll assume that you have at least one or more MIDI instruments at your disposal, each set to one MIDI channel, or that you have one or more multitimbral instruments with each sound set to one MIDI channel. These days, the normal way to work with MIDI is to have MIDI Thru activated in Cubase SX and Local Off selected in your MIDI instruments. By working like this, everything you play during recording will be 'echoed' back out again on the MIDI output and channel selected for the recording track. To achieve this, go to the File menu and open the 'Preferences' dialog box (MIDI page) and make sure that 'MIDI Thru Active' is selected.

Before you start a new recording, and before you start to create a MIDI track, you'll need to open a new Project window. What you'll get is an empty default screen with a number of track options for you to define. Don't worry about the default labels – you can set up your tracks however you want to. To create a MIDI track, select 'Add Track' from the Project menu and then, from the

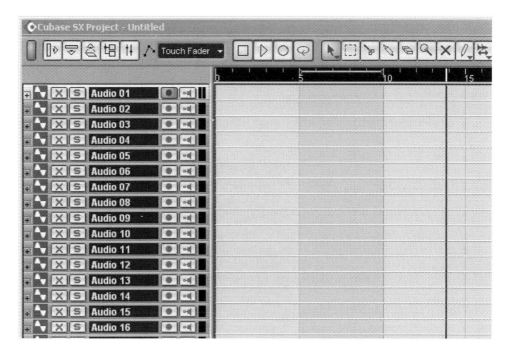

The Cubase SX Project window

submenu that appears, select 'MIDI' and Bob's your uncle – a MIDI track is
added to the Track list.

Adding a track to the Track list

OK, now you'll need to select MIDI inputs for tracks in the Inspector, to the left
of the track list in the Project window. To set the MIDI input for a particular
track, pull down the 'In' pop-up menu in the Track list and select your desired
input. Available MIDI inputs will be listed, and the items shown on the menu
will depend wholly on the type of MIDI interface you're using. You can, of
course, set each track's MIDI input independently.

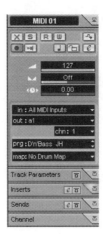

Selecting a MIDI input

Start the MIDI track recording by clicking the corresponding button in the Track list. When the track is record enabled, MIDI Thru is automatically activated, although it can also be set in the Inspector. Once you've done this, try playing a few notes on your MIDI instrument to test the level meter in the Track list and make sure that the MIDI signal is being received loud and clear. If it's not, go back and check that you've set up your MIDI system correctly, as described earlier. If you still have no luck, you'll have to enter the dark and arcane world of MIDI cables.

Once you're satisfied with your sound and signal, set the MIDI output for the track you want to record on by pulling down the 'Out' pop-up menu in the Track list and selecting the output where your chosen MIDI device is connected. Again, available MIDI outputs will be shown, depending on what type of MIDI interface you're using, your system set-up, etc. To actually set the MIDI channel for a track, use the MIDI 'Chn' pop-up menu in the Track list. (Incidentally, if you set the track's MIDI channel to 'Any', it will transmit MIDI on the channels that were used by the MIDI instrument you were playing while recording.)

Selecting a MIDI channel

Everyone will have a different set of MIDI instruments, so I won't go into any great detail concerning wiring and settings. However, to select different sounds, you can send Program Change messages to your MIDI device by clicking the 'Prg' value field in the Track list. You'll find that Program Change messages give access to 128 program locations, and if your MIDI instruments have more than 128 programs, Bank Select messages (set in the 'Bnk' value field) allow you to select different banks, each containing a number of programs. Once you've made your selection, be sure to play a few notes on your MIDI instrument to make sure that your selected sound program is correct, or at least what you had in mind.

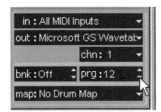

Changing a MIDI sound via the 'Prg' drop-down menu

Now you can get down to recording, which is fairly straightforward. After you've finished, you'll have a part containing MIDI events in your Project window. Before you start, though, make sure that you set the Metronome for an appropriate pre-count and click track.

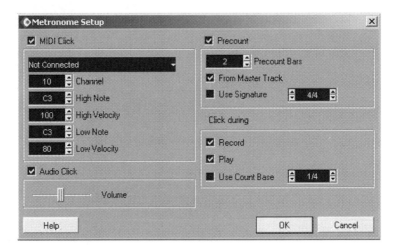

Setting metronome parameters

Set the pre-count for an appropriate number of bars to give you a reasonable lead-in before your song actually starts to be recorded. (You'll also need to set your key signature and tempo to whatever settings you want for your song in the Transport panel.)

Selecting tempo and key signature

Before you start recording, make sure that the Click button is activated so that the guide click track will play through your speakers or MIDI instrument. You should probably also activate Punch In/Out on the Transport panel.

You'll want your recording to start at the cursor position, so pull down the Transport menu and make sure that 'Start Record At Left Locator' is deselected. Place the Project cursor at the position where you wish to begin recording, then activate Record on the Transport panel and play a few notes on your MIDI instrument. As I mentioned earlier, when you've finished recording, a MIDI part containing all of your MIDI events will be created in the Project window. Once you've finished recording, click the Record Enable button in the area to the left of the track so that it goes dark.

To play back what you've just recorded, move the Project cursor to the beginning of the recorded MIDI part either by clicking on the Ruler or by using the Rewind button on the Transport panel. Then, just like with a normal tape recorder, simply click the Play button on the Transport panel and your recording will be played back. When you've listened to your work of genius for long enough, click the Stop button on the Transport panel. As I said earlier, instead of moving the Project cursor manually each time you want to play back a section, you can use the Cycle button on the Transport panel to get Cubase to play back your recorded parts and events repeatedly, over and over again. All you need to do is click on a MIDI part to make sure it's selected, pull down the Transport menu and select 'Locators To Selection', then click the Cycle button on the Transport panel so that it lights up, move the Project cursor to the beginning of the recorded part and click Play. Once playback starts, when the Project cursor reaches the end of the recording at the right locator, it will immediately jump back to the left locator and continue to play.

TIP

When you record MIDI in Cycle mode, what you actually end up with will depend on which Cycle Record mode is selected on the Transport panel. If you've selected 'Mix' for each completed lap, everything you record is added to what was previously recorded in the same part. You might find this particularly useful for building up rhythm patterns or drum parts. If you've selected 'Overwrite' for each completed lap, everything you record will replace whatever you previously recorded in the same part.

quantizing

A real plus with programs like Cubase SX is that, once you've record a track, you can quantize it to sort out any timing discrepancies in your playing. Essentially, quantizing pulls together all of those various rogue notes that you might have misplayed while recording and tightens up your timing to match your desired quantize setting.

To set the desired quantize value, go to the MIDI menu and select 'Quantize Setup'.

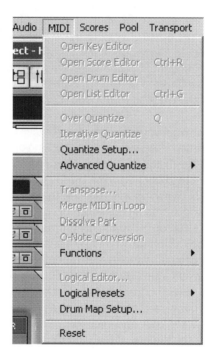

Selecting quantize functions

You will then be presented with a dialog box like that shown at the top of the next page in which you can select quantize values for your music. Whatever values you select will remain valid until you change them, and you can continue to record as many more tracks set to this value as you like. Also, if AutoQuantize is activated on the Transport panel (via the AQ button), the notes you record will automatically be quantized according to the current quantize settings.

recording audio

Essentially, recording audio in Cubase SX isn't all that dissimilar to recording MIDI, in terms of pure logistics, and since this book is essentially designed as a quick start, I won't go into any great details about the arcane world of Windows audio-hardware set-ups and input/output configurations. Each musician chooses

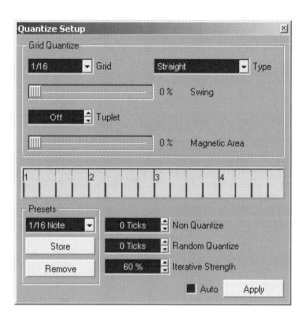

The 'Quantize Setup' dialog box

his or her own preferred studio set-up and kit, and to this end I can only advise (again) that you read all of the documentation that comes with your soundcard, mixer, etc, and follow their instructions meticulously. This means that, before I tell you how to record some audio, I'll assume that you've installed and set up your audio hardware, that your audio source (ie mixer, tape recorder, etc) is properly connected to the inputs of the audio hardware and that the outputs of your audio hardware are connected to equipment that will allow you to listen to the recorded audio during playback. I will also assume that you're monitoring your audio source externally so that you can listen to your audio source before it gets recorded into Cubase SX. (Typical set-ups were described earlier, in Chapter 3.)

As with recording MIDI, before you can start recording audio, you'll need to open a new Project window. To do this, pull down the File menu and select 'New Project' and a dialog will appear listing a number of project templates. Ensure that 'Empty' is selected and then click 'OK'. A 'File' dialog box will appear allowing you to specify a location for the Project folder, which will contain all of the files related to your project. This folder will then be created on your hard drive and an empty Project window will appear. At this point, you can set various criteria for your project, such as sample rate and resolution. However, for purposes of simplicity, use the default settings for now.

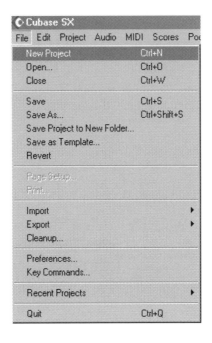

Opening a new project

To create an audio track to record on, simply pull down the Project menu and select 'Add Track'. A submenu will appear listing the various types of tracks available in Cubase SX, and since here you'll be recording audio, select 'Audio' to make an empty audio track appear in your Project window.

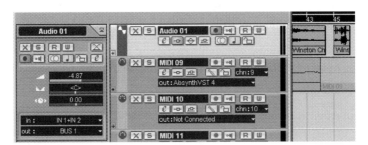

Creating an audio track

Before you can start recording, you'll need to decide whether you want to record in stereo or mono. To make this selection, click the Stereo/Mono switch in the area to the left of the audio track. For example, to make your chosen track stereo, click the button so that it lights up and shows a double circle.

Selecting a stereo track

The next thing you'll need to do is activate and route all of your various inputs.
To do this, simply pull down the Devices menu and select 'VST Inputs'. In the
window that pops up, you'll see lists of all audio inputs on your audio hardware,
enabling you to turn various inputs on or off. From this list, find the input pair
to which you've connected your audio source and click on it to make sure that
its On button in the Active column is...well, on.

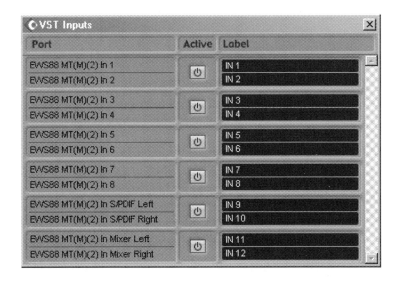

Activating VST inputs

Now close the VST Inputs window and select 'Mixer' from the Devices menu.
This opens Cubase SX's Mixer window, which is used for setting levels, pans
and everything you'd set on a hardware mixer. The Mixer contains a channel
strip for each audio, MIDI and group track in the Project window, so in theory
you should see a single strip of stereo audio channels. Pull down the Input
pop-up menu at the top of this strip to determine which audio input should
be routed to the audio channel for recording. When you select the input pair
to which you've connected your audio source, that audio source will then be

routed to the audio channel so that it can be recorded on the audio track. For the moment, just leave the Mixer window open.

A channel input in the Mixer

OK, the next thing you need to do is to make sure your input level's not too high so that you don't run into clipping. To do this, click the Record Enable button, located next to the fader on the Mixer channel strip. When this button is lit, the level meter will show the input level, as opposed to the level of the playback signal. As you can see here, record enabling the track can be done in the Mixer or in the Track list.

Activating Record Enable status in the Mixer (left) and the Track list (right)

Now, when you activate your audio source, you'll see the level meters reacting. Try to adjust the output level of your audio source so that the meters go as high as possible without going up to 0.0dB, then check the numeric peak-level indicator above the meter in the channel strip.

TIP

It's usually good practice to keep the Transport panel positioned at the bottom of your screen, below your Project window, as this means that you'll always have access to controls that you'll be using quite often.

Before you begin recording, you'll probably want to click on the Stop button and engage the Cycle function, and you'll also need to click in the Ruler (that black timeline above the track in the Project window) at the position where you want to start recording. When you click here, the Project cursor - a black vertical line - is automatically moved to that position, and recording will start from here.

The Cubase SX Project cursor

You can now start recording. Click on the Record button on the Transport panel and the Project cursor will start moving. Play your instrument and, during the recording process, a rectangle will appear covering the recorded area. This is your *recorded audio event*. When you're done, click the Stop button on the Transport panel and Cubase SX will calculate a waveform image of your recording and display it in the audio event.

Audio events in the Project window

To play back your recorded audio track, move the Project cursor to the beginning of the recorded audio event, either by clicking in the ruler or by using the Rewind button on the Transport panel. Then simply click the Play button on the Transport panel and you can listen to your performance. At the risk of restating the obvious, when you're done, click the Stop button on the Transport panel.

You can, of course, carry on and continue recording audio on the same track or on a new track. Indeed, in Cubase SX, it's possible to record audio events that overlap each other, although only the visible events (ie the events at the top) will be heard when you play back.

You'll probably want to record additional tracks and play your existing track while you do so. To do this, create a new audio track by going to the Add Track submenu in the Project menu and choosing either stereo or mono by using the Stereo/Mono switch in the area to the left of the track. Proceed as before and then, in the Project window, click on the new track's Record Enable button. (Always make sure that the Record Enable button for the first track is disabled, though, or you'll find you're recording on both tracks at the same time, which could be disastrous.) Now move the Project cursor to the desired start position and click on the Record button on the Transport panel. While you're recording, the first audio track is also played back.

As I mentioned earlier, you don't have to worry if you decide that you don't like what you've just recorded; you can delete it easily by selecting Undo from the Edit menu. When you do this, the event you've just created will be removed from the Project window and the audio clip in the Pool will be moved to the Trash folder, but the recorded audio file won't be removed from the hard disk. However, since their corresponding clips are moved to the Trash folder, you can delete the files by opening the Pool and selecting Empty Trash from the Pool menu.

TIP

Audio files can be huge, so be aware of the sort of real estate you'll be occupying. As an example, for each minute of audio recording at 44.1kHz mono, you'll burn through around 5Mb of hard-disk space for each channel. That means that, if you want to record continuously on a measly four channels for a miserly three minutes, you'll still need a humungous 60Mb of free hard-disk space. Keep this in mind when you start thinking about using a lot of real instruments or live vocals.

troubleshooting

Although I know I've said it before, when you get into full-blown production, recording digital audio can be a bit like trying to perform an ancient magic spell from a dodgy modern translation of some obscure and dusty grimoire. All the symbols are probably there, the proper ingredients and accoutrements are readily available, but the phrasing and procedural order for completing the great work might have got a bit muddled and obscured along the way. If in the course of your recording session you find yourself confronted by a panoply of unexpected or unwanted demons, just draw a protective circle around your PC and associated kit and ask yourself the following riddles:

- Are your cables and connections faulty, or is it the input signal itself? Is the sound source switched on and active?

- Have you tested your audio card to make sure that it's installed correctly? Could there be some sort of impedance mismatch between your source audio signal and the soundcard?

- Have you inadvertently confused the left and right inputs on your soundcard, and have you chosen the correct input on the selected audio track?

Food for thought or fuel for paranoia? The choice is yours. However, after all that, you should have managed to lay down a few tracks. If, by chance, you've experienced any additional problems, particularly with recording audio, even after trying the various tips mentioned, it's all probably due to the savage and inexplicable intervention of gremlins lurking in the range of parameters related to the audio hardware you happen to be using. But don't despair – the best way to get the sound you want from Cubase SX is to continue to experiment and try out functions as and when you feel you need them. As for all those manuals that came with your soundcard, mixer, MIDI kit, etc, just bung them in the loo and peruse them at your leisure.

chapter 5

studio session 2: MIDI and audio

O K, so far you've hopefully learned how to record some audio and MIDI tracks and you should have a general feel for navigating around Cubase SX's main windows. But, like working in a traditional recording studio, the whole creative process doesn't stop there. Once you've got a few basic tracks down, you then need to start thinking about things like the mix – layering instruments, cutting up sections, sorting out timing and adding various effects that will ultimately allow you to create the perfect finished mix. Cubase SX provides an impressive assortment of virtual mixing consoles and effects racks that include sophisticated EQ controls, adjustable reverb, delay, chorus and other fun toys for achieving the exact sound and feel you're looking for.

An important thing to remember with digital recording is that the whole concept of multitrack mixing can't really be separated from the rest of the recording process. In the digital studio, all those neatly packaged tasks common to traditional studios become somewhat blurred so that, in a sense, you're usually building your mix and final sound in a much more fluid and flexible manner. Ideally, this will allow for more artistic control at each step in the process. And best of all, if it's your PC, you're not paying for studio time by the hour.

Like so many other tools, the mixer windows in Cubase SX have been morphed into a brand new Track Mixer incorporating some of the best features of Nuendo's mixer while pushing the overall functionality that little bit further. The Track Mixer is laid out more like a traditional studio console and looks very little like the mixers in previous versions of Cubase. If you're familiar with earlier versions of Cubase, you'll notice that each channel on the mixer now corresponds to a track on the Project window, with the top-to-bottom ordering of tracks echoed in a militaristic left-to-right formation in the Track Mixer. You no longer have separate mixer windows for MIDI and audio channels, since the Track Mixer now displays the lot in one place. You can configure the new mixer's appearance nearly any way you desire, and the new Extended View

The Cubase SX Mixer window

allows you to set up inserts, sends and built-in EQ from the main Mixer window. In SX, you actually get five Extended Views, providing either eight inserts, eight sends or four sets of EQ controls, and you can display these controls either as knobs or faders, depending on your preference. Even the faders themselves have been narrowed to conserve space.

As you can see from the illustration above, the Mixer window is very similar in appearance to a conventional hardware console, with a level fader for each audio and MIDI channel strip. The Mixer contains the same number of channels as the number of audio and MIDI tracks present in each current project, and along with each channel's level fader you'll also find a level meter which indicates the signal level of audio events on the corresponding audio track during playback. As a point of reference, keep in mind that with MIDI tracks the meters show velocity levels, not signal levels. Apart from the usual audio, MIDI and group channels, you'll also be able to work with any activated ReWire or VST instrument channels, which are also shown in the Mixer.

mixing MIDI

To mix MIDI tracks, your MIDI instruments have to respond to volume and pan messages, and if they happen to support Roland's GS extension of General MIDI, or Yamaha's XG, you'll be able to control a whole range of other parameters such as effects, filters and envelopes. While MIDI tracks are also shown in the Mixer and basic mixer operations such as setting level and pan, using muting and soloing and automation are the same for both audio and MIDI channel strips, it's still worth checking out the relevant chapter in the operating manual for descriptions of MIDI mixing specifics.

OK, so each audio, MIDI and group channel track in the Project window is also represented by a channel strip in the Mixer, which you can open simply by selecting it from the Devices menu. You can also specify which types of channel to show or hide in the Mixer by accessing additional control bars or menus by clicking the arrow on the top bar of each column.

You can also do this by using the 'Channel Type Show/Hide' indicators at the bottom of the Common panel, which will be lit for visible channel types. Show or hide the desired channel type in the Mixer by clicking on the corresponding channel-type indicator, as shown below.

The leftmost column of buttons on the channel strip – shown at the top of the next page – is called the Common panel and has all your controls for setting things like pan control, mute and solo and channel automation, as well as an edit button, bypass inserts, disable sends and monitor and record enable buttons. Directly above the fader to the right of the pan control is the MIDI input source pop-up and directly to the right of the fader is the level/velocity meter. At the bottom of each fader pod you'll find the MIDI output routing pop-up.

Moving onto the Master section, which usually appears on the left of the mixer, you'll find controls for the master volume, master level meters, and at the bottom the master mono/stereo switch, output routing pop-ups and automation controls. The Master section allows you to control the output level of the main output bus, and with the Mixer in Extended mode, the Master section will also contain the master-effect slots. (This section can be shown or hidden in the Mixer by clicking the Show Master button in the Common panel.) Directly above the Master mixer you'll find the master-effects slots as well.

The Cubase SX channel strip

Steinberg has designed the Mixer panel to look and feel as close to any real-world console as possible within a virtual environment. So, like in the real world, you slide the faders to increase or decrease volume, and each channel has a Mute button to silence the output of selected tracks and a Solo button which silences the outputs of all other tracks shown on the Mixer. As mentioned earlier, all of these controls are now more or less standardised for both MIDI and audio in Cubase SX.

The Master section

Remember, the level meters for MIDI channels don't show volume levels. Instead, they indicate the velocity values of the notes played back on MIDI tracks, so if you pull down a fader for a MIDI channel that's playing, your meter will still show the same level, although the actual volume will change because the connected MIDI device is set to respond to MIDI volume.

When working with MIDI, use the Track Control effect to adjust parameters on GS- or XG-compatible MIDI devices. As I mentioned in Chapter 4, the Roland GS and Yamaha XG protocols are extensions of the General MIDI standard, providing more sounds and better control of various instrument settings. If your own instrument is compatible with GS or XG, the Track Control box allows you to adjust sounds and effects in your instrument from within Cubase SX. At the top of the Track Control window, you'll find a pop-up menu where you can select any of the available control panels. Users of previous versions of Cubase will notice a slight change in the modes available, which include:

- **XG Effect And Sends** - Effect sends and various sound-control parameters for use with instruments compatible with Yamaha's XG standard

- **XG Global** - Global settings affecting all channels for instruments compatible with Yamaha's XG standard

- **GS Basic Controls** - Effect sends and various sound-control parameters for use with instruments compatible with Roland's GS standard

- **Off** - No control parameters available

The Track Control box

When you're mixing, remember that, if you have several MIDI tracks/Mixer channels set to the same MIDI channel and routed to the same MIDI output, any volume settings you make for one of these tracks or channels will also affect all other Mixer channels set to the same MIDI channel or output combination. This also applies to things like pan settings.

mixing audio

Audio-related channels – which include audio, group, VST instrument and ReWire channels – all have essentially the same channel-strip layout on the mixer. However, since audio inputs are never routed to group or VST instrument channels, audio tracks – or *disk channels*, as they're otherwise known – also have an Input Source pop-up menu as well as being equipped with Record Enable and Monitor buttons. You'll also notice that VST instrument channels have an additional Edit (e) button for opening the instrument's control panel.

As well as the controls described earlier in this chapter, audio-related channels include three additional Insert, EQ and Send indicators and Bypass buttons. If, for example, an insert or send effect or EQ module is activated for a channel, the corresponding button here is lit. (Usually, the effect indicators will be blue and the EQ indicator green.) If you click these buttons when they're lit, the corresponding EQ or effects section will be bypassed, indicated by the button turning yellow. Clicking the button again will deactivate the bypass.

Channel strip functions

In all audio-related channels, the faders control the volume of the channels before they're routed directly or via a group channel to a stereo output bus, with separate faders for the left and right outputs. Use the Master Gain fader in the Mixer to determine the output level of the Master bus. Fader settings are displayed numerically below the faders, in decibels for audio channels and in MIDI volume (taking the range of values from 0 to 127) for MIDI channels.

If you want to make fine volume adjustments, hold down [Shift] when you move the faders. If you hold down [Ctrl] and click on a fader, it will automatically be set to 0.0dB for audio channels or MIDI volume 100 for MIDI channels.

In Cubase SX, the Audio Output bus faders usually move either together or in tandem. However, if you deactivate the Fader Link switch or hold down [Alt], you can move each one independently. You can also use the faders to set up a volume balance between the audio and MIDI channels, allowing you to mix manually by adjusting the faders and other controls during playback. A bit later in the book, I'll be showing you how to automate levels and...well, just about everything else in the Mixer.

When you play back your audio in Cubase SX, the level meters in the Mixer register levels for each audio channel. If the peak level of the audio goes above 0dB, the numeric level indicator will then show a positive value above this mark. Cubase SX uses 32-bit floating-point processing internally, which means that your headroom is virtually limitless; even though you're working in a digital environment, your signals can go way beyond 0dB without introducing distortion. So, for the most part, having levels higher than 0dB for individual channels and groups isn't a serious problem in itself, and your audio quality won't be degraded. However, this isn't the case for the buses shown in the VST Outputs window, including the Master bus, which can also be shown in the Mixer.

In comparison, in the output buses, the floating-point audio is converted to the resolution of the audio hardware, and in the audio domain the maximum level is 0dB. Levels higher than this will definitely cause the indicators above the meters for each bus to light up, showing that clipping is taking place and that you're producing real digital distortion, which should be avoided at all costs.

TIP

While overdriving digital audio is generally to be discouraged, in some dance and electronica mixes you'll find that artists have actually done it on purpose to create strangely textured distortion effects. So, as with most things in Cubase SX, just because someone says you shouldn't do it, that doesn't mean you can't give it a try if it seems like a good idea. As they say, serendipity – or even a blatant mistake – can occasionally add an unexpected and positively creative element that makes a recording unique.

Within the Channel Settings window, you can apply Equalisation, Send Effects and Insert Effects to your mix, and you can also copy complete channel settings and apply them to any other channel. As I mentioned earlier, pressing the Edit

The Cubase SX Channel Settings window

(e) button on an audio channel in the Mixer – as well as in the Inspector for each audio track – will give you access to this window.

When opened, the VST Channel Settings window contains the Common panel, a duplicate of the Mixer channel strip, a section with eight insert-effect slots, four EQ modules and an associated EQ-curve display and a section with eight effect sends. Each channel has its own channel settings, although you can view them all in the same window if you wish. (Remember, though, that all channel settings are applied to both sides of a stereo channel.) Selecting a track in the Project window automatically selects the corresponding channel in the Mixer and vice versa, and if a Channel Settings window is open, this will immediately switch to show the settings for the selected channel. This means that you can have a single Channel Settings window open in a convenient position on the screen and use it for all of your EQ and channel effect settings. Alternatively, you can select a channel manually and change what's shown in the open Channel Settings window.

When mixing, you'll eventually work out a number of cool settings that give you the precise sound or texture you're looking for. When this happens, you'll also find it useful to be able to copy all of those channel settings and paste them onto another channel. In Cubase SX, you can do this with all types of audio channel – for example, you could copy EQ settings from an

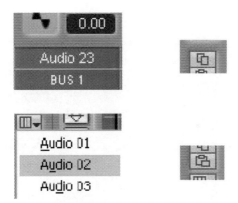

Controls in the Channel Settings window.
Clockwise from top left: Channel Selection,
Copy button, Paste button, Common panel selection

audio channel and apply these to a group or VST instrument channel to give your mix a consistent sound or feel. To use this feature, simply select the channel you want to copy settings from by clicking its Channel Name field and then clicking the Copy button in the Common panel. Then select the channel to which you want to copy the settings and click the Paste button. And if that isn't clever enough, you can even copy channel settings from stereo channels and paste them into mono channels and vice versa.

OK, let's have a little play with some of the mixing controls. When you record in stereo, you need to determine where in the mix various instruments and vocals will actually appear and how their sound will relate to the rest of the instrumentation. This involves panning a particular channel to a position somewhere between the left and right side of the stereo spectrum. For stereo audio channels, the Pan control governs the overall balance between the left and right channels. As a general rule of thumb, most producers suggest panning bass instruments, bass drums and usually the snare to the centre of the mix. Toms and overhead microphones can be spread from left to right, but don't pan them too hard or it will sound particularly weird. Things like lead vocals tend to work best near the centre of the mix, unless you've got two strong vocals or significant harmonies that you want to spread, while backing vocals can be spread a lot more or dropped further back in the mix. With effects, unless you're trying for something specific, it's probably best to keep outputs from effects such as stereo reverb panned hard left and right to ensure that they have the same level in the mix.

Click on the blue line in the Pan control box above the fader and drag to the left or right to change a sound's position in a mix

 TIP

It's always a good idea to check that your mix is in mono to make sure that the way you've used stereo effects hasn't changed the balance of the overall mix in an adverse manner.

Have a play with the Pan controls and listen to the affect they have on your overall sound. If you want to make particularly fine pan adjustments, hold down [Shift] when you move the pan control, or select the central pan position by holding down [Ctrl] and clicking on the pan control. With audio channels, the output-bus faders determine the levels on each side in the stereo output, and you should also remember that there are no pan controls for VST output buses or the Master bus. With MIDI channels, meanwhile, the Pan control sends out MIDI pan messages, and the results that you achieve will depend entirely on how your MIDI instrument is set to respond to these.

While we're here, why not have a play with the Mute and Solo buttons as well? Have a go at silencing one or several of your audio or MIDI channels. You'll find that clicking the Mute button silences the selected channel while clicking the Solo button mutes all other channels. Solo'd channels are indicated by a lit Solo

Solo (left) and Mute (right) selected on two different channels

button and also by the lit Global Solo indicator on the Common panel. (Of course, several channels can be solo'd at the same time.) If you press [Ctrl] and click the Solo button for a channel, any other solo'd channels will automatically be un-solo'd, while clicking a Solo button while holding down [Alt] will activate 'Solo Group' for that channel. (You can always un-mute or un-solo all channels by clicking the Mute or Solo indicators in the Common panel.)

mixing tips

I'll be telling you more about these and other mixing features in a bit more detail in Chapter 8, 'Studio Session 4: Mixing', but while we're on the subject of mixing it's always worth pointing out that a really good mix always starts with a good performance and a well-thought-out arrangement. Despite all the digital magic, if you're not in tune and in time, you'll have one hell of a tedious job building a new and workable performance out of the scrapheap. Yes, you can do a lot to improve small errors, but it's always worth trying to sort out the major problems in the performance at the recording stage rather than trying to fix absolutely everything in the mix. If your mix includes sequenced instruments, it's true that MIDI gives you the opportunity to change sounds right up until the last moment. However, it's still best to have a clear idea of the sound you want before you start since, while modern synths like the Korg Triton sound so extraordinarily rich and impressive on their own, they can give you almost too much choice, and their cool presets can take up all the space in a mix, swamping everything else.

While you're experimenting with the various mixing facilities in Cubase SX, there are a few production guidelines that are worth remembering each time you're working through a recording and mixing session. The simple things are obvious, such as making sure that your microphone placement is optimal and working with your acoustic environment, as well as using the right microphone for the job.

Also, it's important not to over-use EQ. Of course, if your mic placement is right, this won't be much of an issue. Think of EQ as a tool with which to improve creatively already well-recorded sounds and a subtle means of balancing those sounds in your mix.

Be aware that long mixing sessions will make your ears go woolly, so don't abuse them with abnormally high monitor volumes. Take plenty of breaks during mixing sessions and remember that Frank Zappa considered coffee and cigarettes food.

Getting a perfect mix isn't an easy task, and many musicians and producers will maintain that a mix is never perfect. Sometimes the more sophisticated your kit, the more difficult it is to get a mix you're satisfied with, and you should always go with your creative instincts rather than with the potential of your equipment. Just remember that it's fine to experiment with functionality, but it's how your music sounds to you and your audience that really matters, not how you managed to produce it.

chapter 6

editing and
manipulating tracks

No matter how experienced or how well rehearsed they are, few musicians can go into a studio and lay down a perfect track first time, every time. Sure, there are exceptions, and probably a lot more who just think they're exceptions, but for the rest of us it's nice to know that, if we don't get something right the first time, we can either do it all over again or, if we're using Cubase SX, get right down inside the song and try to fix it. One of the best features of Cubase SX is that, in most instances, you can effectively edit your song and its overall sound visually. So far I've taken you through some of the main techniques involved in getting your tracks recorded at the arrangement level, but once you've recorded your parts you can then begin to use Cubase SX's powerful tools to carry out a wide range of editing functions that will help you manipulate your tracks and arrangement until your song sounds exactly the way you want it to.

As I mentioned in Chapter 4, all of the parts that you create in the Project window can be moved freely between tracks and duplicated as well as split, joined, lengthened, shortened, grouped and much more, even while the music is being played. Cubase also provides a number of specific editors that allow you to look at and work with the contents of each part in detail. When you're using the tools in Cubase SX for editing parts and events, you can in many cases apply additional functions by pressing modifier keys - for example, pressing [Alt] and dragging with the Pencil tool creates a copy of the dragged event or part - so let's have a look at the various default modifier keys available. (Remember, you can customise these if need be by going to the Preferences dialog box in the Editing menu and selecting 'Tool Modifiers'.) For the sake of convenience, while discussing editing in the Project window, unless explicitly stated, all descriptions listed below as 'events' apply to both events and parts.

selecting parts and events

To select an event, choose the Arrow tool and access the Select submenu on the Edit menu. You'll be presented with the following options:

- **All** - Selects all events in the Project window

- **None** - Deselects all events

- **In Loop** - Selects all events that are partly or wholly between the left and right locators

- **From Start To Cursor** - Selects all events that begin to the left of the Project cursor

- **From Cursor To End** - Selects all events that end to the right of the Project cursor

- **All On Selected Tracks** - Selects all events on the selected track

- **Select Event** - Available in the Sample Editor

- **Left/Right Selection** and **Side To Cursor** - These two functions are used only for range-selection editing

If you want to, say, select all events on a track, simply right-click in its Track list and choose 'Select All Events' from the pop-up menu. You can also use the arrow keys on your keyboard to select the closest event to the left, right, above or below. It's also useful to know that, if you press [Shift] and use the arrow keys, the current selection will be kept, allowing you to select several events. And if the option 'Auto Select Events Under Cursor' is activated in the Preferences dialog box on the Editing page, all events currently touched by the Project cursor will be selected automatically. This can be helpful when you're rearranging your project, as it allows you to select whole sections on all tracks simply by moving the Project cursor. It's also possible to select ranges, regardless of the event and track boundaries, by using the Range Selection tool.

duplicating events

To copy an event, hold down [Alt] and drag the selected event to the desired new position. (If Snap is activated, this will determine the exact position at which your copy will be placed.) If you hold down [Ctrl] as well, your direction of movement will be restricted to either horizontal or vertical axes, which means that, if you drag an event vertically, it can't be moved horizontally at the same time. Audio and MIDI parts can also be duplicated by pressing [Alt] + [Shift] and dragging to create a *shared copy* of the part. However, be warned that, if you edit the contents of a shared copy, all other shared copies of the same part will automatically be edited in the same way. I should also point out that, when you duplicate audio *events*, the copies are always shared, which means that shared copies of audio events always refer to the same audio clip. You can always convert a shared copy to a real copy by selecting 'Convert To Real Copy' from the Edit menu, which creates a new version of the clip that can be edited independently and which is then added to the Pool. As you might expect, selecting 'Duplicate' from the Edit menu creates a copy of the selected event and places it directly after the original. If several events are selected, all of these are copied as a single entity while maintaining the relative distance between the events. Selecting 'Fill Loop' from the Edit menu creates a number of copies starting at the left locator and ending at the right locator.

moving events

To move an individual event, just click on it in the Project window and drag it to its new position. When you select a number of events, they will all be moved, maintaining their relative positions. Remember, you can drag events only to tracks of the same type, and if Snap is activated, this will determine the positions to which you can move the events.

You'll probably notice that there's a slight delay in Cubase's response when you move an event by dragging. Steinberg maintains that this helps you avoid accidentally moving events when you click on them in the Project window. To prove this, they allow you to adjust the delay via the 'Drag Delay' setting in the Preferences dialog. Functions available include:

- **Move To Cursor** - Moves the selected event to the Project cursor's position. If there are several selected events on the same track, the first event will start at the cursor and the following events will be lined up end-to-start after the first.

- **Move To Origin** - Moves the selected events to their original positions, ie where they were originally recorded.

- **Move To Front/Move To Back** - This function doesn't actually change the position of the events, but instead it moves the selected events to the front or back, respectively. It can be useful if you happen to have overlapping events and you want to see one that's partially obscured. This is particularly important for audio events, since only the visible sections of events will be played back. Moving an obscured audio event to the front or moving an obscuring event to back allows you to hear the whole event on playback.

splitting events

You can split events in the Project window by selecting the Scissors tool and then clicking on the event you want to split. Again, if Snap is activated, it will determine the exact position of the split. Alternatively, you can split events by selecting 'Split At Cursor' from the Edit menu, which splits the selected events at the position of the Project cursor. If no events are selected, all events on all tracks that are intersected by the Project cursor will be split.

If you split a MIDI part so that the split position intersects one or several MIDI notes, the result will depend on whether or not the option 'Split MIDI Events' (found in the Preferences dialog box in the MIDI Function Parameters) is activated. If it is, the intersected notes will be split, creating new notes at the beginning of the second part. If it's deactivated, the notes will remain in the first part but will appear to stick out at the end of the part.

joining events

Clicking on an event with the Glue tool joins an event together with the next event on the track. The result is a part containing the two events. However, if you first split an event and then glue the two sections together again, without moving or editing them first, they'll magically become a single event again. So keep in mind that glueing can create a single event only if the two events are lined up end-to-start and play a continuous section of the same clip.

resizing events

Resizing events means moving their start or end positions individually. In Cubase SX, there are three types of resizing modes available, and to select one you just need to select the Arrow tool and then click again on the Arrow icon on the toolbar. This will open a pop-up menu from which you can select one of the resizing mode options. The icon on the toolbar will change shape to indicate the selected resizing mode. Options available from the menu include:

- **Normal Sizing** – The contents of the event stay fixed and the start or end point of the event is moved to reveal more or less of the contents

- **Sizing Moves Contents** – The contents follow the moved start or end of the event

- **Sizing Applies Time Stretch** – The contents are time-stretched to fit the new event length

Resizing events

removing events

Sometimes you just want to get rid of stuff you've recorded and start again. In Cubase SX, to remove an event from the Project window, you can either click on the event with the Eraser tool, you can select the event and press [Backspace] or you can choose 'Delete' from the Edit menu. If you use the Erase tool and press [Alt], all of the following events on the same track will be deleted.

editors

OK, so the Project Browser provides a list-based representation of the project that allows you to view and edit all events on all tracks. However, there are also a number of more specific editors available for when you want to work on elements of your project in more particular detail. Previous versions of Cubase have all included the now familiar Key, List, Drum and Score Editors, and all of these have survived the transition to Cubase SX with little or no major alterations. If anything, they've all probably benefited from SX's all-pervasive, system-wide multiple undo functionality. The Score Editor now looks like the advanced version that appeared only in Cubase VST/32, and most of the visual aspects of your score can be configured via the Score menu.

You'll find that the score settings in the main Preferences are reserved for general settings in the Score Editor, since any changes you make here will be non-specific. Of the lot, the most significant new feature is the ability to display multiple controller lanes simultaneously in the Key and Drum Editors. You'll find this particularly useful for editing things like pitch-bend information, as it means that you can now keep all of the note velocities visible on screen at the same time. The Mastertrack Editor of previous incarnations is now known as the Tempo Track Editor and provides similar functionality, in most cases, for all things to do with tempo and time-signature changes. Meanwhile, the Master button still appears on the Transport panel and shows you whether or not the Master tempo or the Rehearsal tempo is on or off, and a new Project browser – nicked directly from Nuendo – has been added to allow you to categorise every element of an entire project – such as audio and MIDI events and automation data – into a neat, database-style format, replacing previous list-based editors.

Although the Pool has been included in most recent versions of Cubase, in SX it has been given a new and improved organisation and set of features, also stolen straight from Nuendo. Previous users of Cubase will notice that the most significant change to the Pool in SX is that there are now three new Audio, Video and Trash folders. Another nice touch is that you can now organise the Pool more clearly by creating nested subfolders within the Audio and Video folders. While this doesn't affect the way in which files are actually stored on your hard disk, it can make locating clips in the Pool a lot easier.

Here's a brief run-down of how each editor operates.

pool

This is where all of your files that belong to a particular project are listed. There's a separate pool for each project, so while you're hopefully, metaphorically waving, not drowning, you can organise, convert and audition clips as well as a variety of other things.

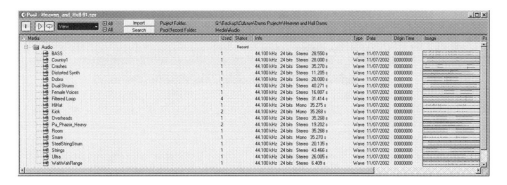

The Pool in Cubase SX

Sample Editor

Here's where you can view and manipulate audio, by cutting and pasting, removing or drawing audio data. If you use the Offline Process History, you can undo changes or revert to the original versions at any point.

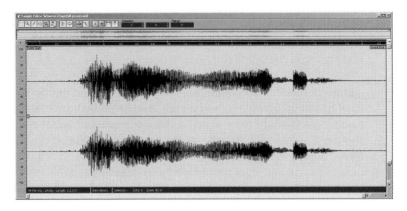

The Sample Editor

MIDI editors

You can do all your editing of MIDI data with the MIDI editors, which include:

Key Editor

This shows the contents of a single MIDI part, with all MIDI notes represented by boxes whose vertical position corresponds to their MIDI note values, and therefore their pitches. The Controller display shows continuous MIDI events, such as controllers or the velocity values of notes, which can be edited or added to with the Pencil tool.

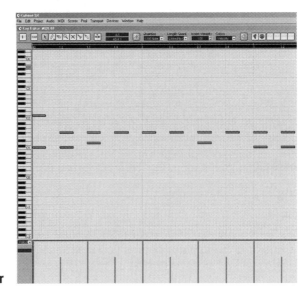

The Key Editor

Score Editor

The Score Editor shows MIDI notes as a musical score and comes with advanced tools and functions to facilitate notation, layout and printing. Unfortunately, for some reason, the Score Editor didn't work properly on the system I was using to test the early-release version – the score would appear, but apparently there was some problem with fonts and I ended up with odd-looking square characters instead of the usual musical notation. I will assume that either there was just some problem with my system or there was a glitch in early releases that Steinberg will get around to sorting out in later versions.

List Editor

The List Editor shows all events in a MIDI part as a list, allowing you to view and edit their properties numerically. The display lists all of the events in the currently selected MIDI part in the order in which they're played back, from top to bottom. You can edit the event properties by using regular value editing.

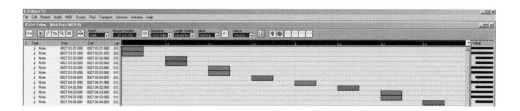

The List Editor

Drum Editor

The Drum Editor is similar to the Key Editor but takes advantage of the fact that, with drum parts, each key corresponds to a separate drum sound. With MIDI, a drum kit is usually a set of different drum sounds, with each sound placed on a separate key – ie different sounds are assigned to different MIDI note numbers so that one key plays a bass-drum sound, another a snare, another a cymbal, etc. Unfortunately, different MIDI instruments often use different key assignments, which can be troublesome if you've programmed a drum pattern using one MIDI device and then want to try it on another; when you switch devices, it's very likely that your snare drum will become a ride cymbal or your hi-hat will turn into a tom, for instance, because the drum sounds are distributed differently in the two instruments and...well, just because MIDI is like that.

To solve this problem and to simplify several aspects of MIDI drum kits, Cubase SX gives you access to drum maps, which basically provide a list of drum sounds with a number of settings for each sound. When you play back a MIDI track with a selected drum map, the MIDI notes are filtered through the drum map before being sent to the MIDI instrument. Among other things, the map determines which MIDI note number is sent out for each drum sound, and therefore which sound is played in the receiving MIDI device.

There's always some variance in the various toolboxes in Cubase SX, and you'll notice in the Drum Editor that there's no Pencil tool. Instead, some imaginative developer decided that we should have a Drumstick tool for inputting and removing notes and a Paint tool with various line and curve modes for painting in several notes in one go or editing controller events. Not only that but there are no Scissors and Glue tools available in the Drum Editor, either.

As in the Key Editor, the mouse-pointer display in the toolbar shows the pitch and position of the pointer, but the pitch is shown as a drum-sound name rather than a note number. The Global Quantize button, meanwhile, will allow you to select which value should be used when Snap is on. (Use the Global Quantize value on the toolbar or the individual quantize values for the drum sounds.) Finally, instead of a Length Quantize setting, you'll find an Insert Length pop-up menu.

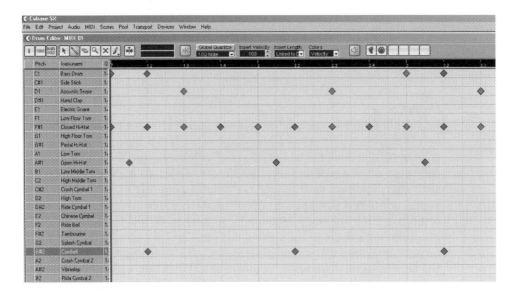

The Drum Editor

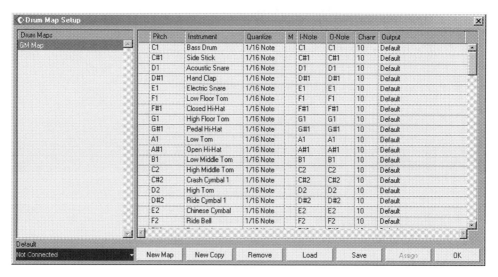

Drum map set-up

Tempo Track Editor

In Cubase SX, you can specify whether each audio and MIDI track should use musical or linear time. Tempo-based tracks follow a tempo, which can either be fixed through the whole project or follow the Tempo track. In the Tempo Track Editor, you can draw curves that determine how the tempo will change over time.

For each audio or MIDI track in Cubase SX, you can specify whether it should be time-based or tempo-based. For tempo-based tracks, the tempo can either be fixed through the whole project (referred to as 'Rehearsal Tempo') or vary over time (called 'Master Tempo'). If you want to switch between rehearsal tempo and master tempo, use the Master button on the Transport panel or in the Tempo Track Editor. (Remember that, when the Master button is activated, the tempo follows the Tempo track, and when it's deactivated the Rehearsal Tempo is used.) The Tempo track also contains time-signature events, and these are always active, regardless of whether Rehearsal mode or Master mode is selected.

using the editors

Experiment with these various editors and notice the variations in the tools available for each. For example, open the Key Editor by double-clicking a MIDI part in the Project window; the Editor window will show the contents of a single part. (Remember that you can have several editors open at the same time.) The main area of the Key Editor is the Note display, which contains a

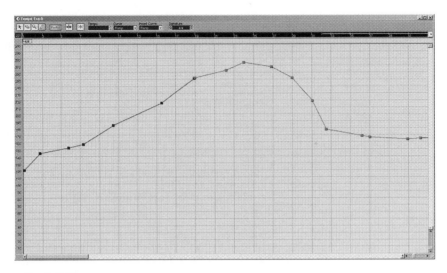

The Tempo Track Editor

grid showing MIDI notes as boxes, with the width of a box corresponding to the note length and its vertical position corresponding to the note number (pitch) so that higher notes appear higher up in the grid. The piano keyboard to the left serves as a guide for finding the right note number. At the bottom of the Key Editor window you'll see the Controller display, used for viewing and editing various values and events, such as velocity.

Note that, when you move the pointer in the Note display, its bar position is indicated in the toolbar and its pitch is indicated both in the toolbar and on the piano keyboard to the left, making it easy to find the right note and insert position. To insert new notes in the Key Editor, select the Pencil tool and click at the desired time position and pitch. If you click just once, the created note will be set to the length determined on the Length Quantize pop-up menu on the toolbar. If you wish, you can create a longer note by clicking and dragging the pointer to the right while pressing the mouse button. The length of the created note will be a multiple of the Length Quantize value and the notes will have the Insert Velocity value set on the toolbar.

The transparency of Cubase SX and its ability to let you edit your music at almost any level and to any degree makes it an exceptionally powerful tool. Essentially, anything that you can do in the Project window relating to playback or recording can also be done in the various editors. And as well as being able to go from the Project window to any editor, you can just as easily go from one editor to another or have several editors open at the same time.

Editing happens in real time, so you can edit while music is playing or even while you're recording. If you don't want to record in real time, you can use step recording to input drum tracks or other instruments one note at a time. For example, the List Edit window allows you to view and edit most of the various event types in all of Cubase SX's different track classes. The columns in the list represent different values, depending on each track's class and the type of event, and you can insert any event type, including notes, as well as set the length of each note manually while you're entering it, just as you would in the Key Edit window. Personally, I find the List Edit window rather daunting, and unless you're involved with recording massive arrangements where editing any type of MIDI event requires an extreme level of detail, you may never even need to use it. While the Key Edit window is more accessible, with its graphic approach, List Edit is probably the province of aspiring sound engineers interested in editing non-note events and sysex (system-exclusive) data. However, unlike the Key Edit window, in List Edit you can edit only one track or selected part at a time, although you can edit audio events and MIDI events in fine detail. Whether or not you ever use it is up to you, and if you're using an external sampler you'll already be doing a lot of this there instead of in Cubase.

However, from a musician's point of view, you'll find both the Drum Edit and Drum Map windows particularly interesting and useful here – you might find, for instance, that the more detailed List Edit-type parameters make more sense. In Cubase, a drum map consists of settings for 128 drum sounds which can be named and set to represent particular drum sounds on your synth, sampler or drum machine. You can have up to 64 drum maps in your song at the same time, allowing you to create several different drum tracks, each with its own drum map. Keep in mind the fact that each drum track uses only one drum map at a time and that, when you've defined a sound, all notes already recorded with that sound appear as diamonds on their particular line in the Note display. Initially, the Drum Map window's pop-up menu will contain only one map, the 'GM Map', although you'll also find a number of drum maps included on the Cubase installation CD-ROM.

For each drum sound, you can define what might seem to be a lot of complex parameters, but for most musicians only two are really important for understanding drum maps: the I-note and O-note values. The I-note is a certain key or MIDI note number used for playing the sound, and setting this value determines which key on your MIDI instrument, drum pad or other device plays the sound. (Keep in mind that two sounds cannot share the same I-note.) The O-note value, meanwhile, is the MIDI note number that the sound actually outputs when the instrument is played by you or the sound is played back by Cubase. Let's say that you have a rack synth with some drum sounds in it but they're spread over the range of the keyboard in a way that's inconvenient for your playing style. You can get around this by setting the O-notes in the drum map so that they match the actual notes that play back the sounds on your instrument. If the instrument plays back the bass drum on the C2 key, you could set the O-note value for the bass-drum sound to just that, C2, so that the instrument plays the bass drum. Now you can rearrange the whole 'drum kit' to suit your fingering just by setting the right I-notes.

While each of the 128 sounds of a MIDI device has a note number, this is neither the I-note nor the O-note value but simply a note number used to sort and keep track of the sounds. This might seem like more than you'd wish to know, but only this 'real' note number is recorded by Cubase. As soon as you open a drum part in another editor, the 'real' note numbers will be revealed. If you open a drum track in the List Edit window, or open a folder track containing drum tracks in the Key Edit window, the notes will be shown with their 'real' note numbers, which could make things rather confusing. Therefore, it's always a good idea to edit drum tracks in Drum Edit only. Like Key Edit, Drum Edit also has a Controller display, but this shows only data for the currently selected sound.

While the Drum Edit window makes it relatively easy to create, edit and generally muck about with percussion patterns and even create parts from scratch with the Drumstick or Brush tools, using a keyboard in real time will usually give you a more natural and realistic feel. Try recording whole sections rather than just a few bars that you can loop by copying and pasting. Also, recording a couple of drum tracks at once can give a more natural sound than a number of tracks recorded separately. Of course, this isn't a hard-and-fast rule, and if you're programming some complex breakbeat or other dance stuff then you might decide to program differently. Finally, when you're creating a new drum map, it's often a good idea to start with a map that's similar to the sort you want, if its available, and simply edit it. After all, re-inventing the wheel is never the most productive result of your creative endeavours.

TIP

In Cubase SX, in order to be allowed into the Pool, files must:

- *be AIFF, WAV, SDII or MP3 format*
- *be uncompressed 16-bit or 24-bit files*
- *have sample rates the same as the one used in your song*
- *be mono or stereo*

AIFF files are most common on the Mac, while WAV files are more common on PCs, and of course you can also import audio files directly into the Project window. If you want to work with MP3 files, keep in mind that these are compressed and can't be played back directly by Cubase. When you import a compressed audio file, Cubase SX creates a copy of the file and converts it to WAV format before importing it. The original compressed file will not be used in the project and the WAV file will be placed in the designated Project Audio folder. Also keep in mind that, while the original MP3 might be quite small, the converted WAV file will definitely be a lot bigger.

OK, I know, Cubase SX is huge and a book purporting to be a fast guide can't possibly cover every feature in absolute detail. And dwelling on geeky tech stuff can be about as dull as the sharp end of a dull thing, particularly for practising musicians. But even if you are a practising musician and not an aspiring sound engineer, a basic understanding of a lot of these features in Cubase SX is important, even if only to allow you to decide not to use some of them. However, as suggested in earlier chapters, in the world of desktop digital recording, even experienced musicians may be seduced into becoming overly preoccupied with the technical details of their MIDI systems and start to forget that the object of the exercise is to create some music. We've all witnessed the sad scene in the recording studio when the musicians wait for hours on end while the newly converted programmer grapples with all kinds of arcane and obscure parameters in the digitally misguided quest for what ostensibly passes for musical perfection.

not fade away

When you're mixing instruments, vocals, etc, you'll find that it's often useful to be able to fade a piece of music down at the end, or even perhaps fade it up at the beginning. Even within the arrangement you might want to fade a particular part in or out of the mix.

Cubase SX lets you apply fades in a couple of different ways. To begin with, you can use the blue fade handles in the upper left and right corners of selected audio events. These can be dragged to create a fade-in or fade-out respectively. When, for example, you're creating a fade-in, the fade is automatically reflected in the shape of the event's waveform, giving you a visual feedback of the result when you drag the fade handle.

Be aware that fades created with the handles are not applied to the audio clip, as such. Instead, Cubase SX seamlessly switches between the fade sections and the actual clip on playback. This means that several events referring to the same audio clip can have different fade curves. This also means that, if you select multiple events and drag the fade handles on one of them, the same fade will be applied to all selected events. You can also edit a fade in the Fade dialog by double-clicking on the fade or by clicking on the event and selecting 'Open Fade Editors' from the Audio menu. This will open two dialogs if the event has both fade-in and fade-out curves, and if you adjust the shape of the fade curve in the Fade dialog, this shape will be maintained when you later adjust the length of the fade. You can make the fade longer or shorter at any time by dragging the handle, even without selecting the event first (ie without handles being visible). Just move the mouse pointer along the fade curve until the cursor turns into a bidirectional arrow, then click and drag. If the option 'Show Event Volume Curves Always' is activated in the Preferences dialog (in 'Event Display' on the Audio page), the fade curves will be shown in all events, regardless of whether or not they're selected. If the option is deactivated, the fade curves are shown only in selected events only.

Handle-type fades can also be created and adjusted with the Range Selection tool by using it to select a section of the audio event. Depending on your selection, you'll create a fade-in if you select a range from the beginning of the event or a fade-out if you select a range that reaches the end of an event. If you select a range encompassing the middle section of an event but reaching neither the start nor the end, both a fade-in and a fade-out will be created outside the selected range. In other words, the fade-in will cover the area from the beginning of the event to the beginning of the selected range, and the fade-out will cover the area from the end of the selected range to the end of the event. Use the 'Adjust Fades To Range' function in the Audio menu to adjust the fade areas according to the selection range. You can select multiple audio events on separate tracks with the Range Selection tool and apply the fade to all of them simultaneously.

fade dialogs

When you edit an existing fade or use the 'Fade In' and 'Fade Out' functions on the Audio menu's Process submenu, the Fade dialog box appears. If you open the Fade dialogs with several events selected, you can adjust the fade curves for all of these events at the same time, which is useful if you want to apply the same type of fade-in to more than one event, for instance. Here's a breakdown of the parameters in the Fade dialog box:

- **Curve Kind** – Determines whether the fade curve should consist of spline curve segments (left button) or linear segments (right button).

- **Fade Display** – Shows the shape of the fade curve. The resulting waveform shape is shown in dark grey, with the current waveform shape in light grey. You can click on the curve to add points and click and drag existing points to change the shape. To remove a point from the curve, drag it outside the display.

- **Restore Button** – Located to the right, above the fade display, this is available only while editing fades by dragging the their handles. Click this to cancel any changes you've made since opening the dialog.

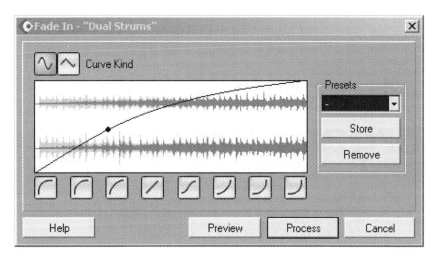

'Fade In' dialog box

- **Curve Shape Buttons** – Give you quick access to some common curve shapes.

- **Default Button** – Clicking this stores the current settings as the default fade, which will be used whenever you create a new fade.

- **Presets** – If you've set up a fade-in or fade-out curve that you might want to apply to other events or clips, you can store it as a preset by clicking the Store button. To apply a stored preset, select it from the pop-up menu. To rename the selected preset, double-click on the name and type in a new one. To remove a stored preset, select it from the pop-up menu and click 'Remove'. Remember that stored fade-in presets will appear only in the 'Fade In' dialog box and fade-out presets only in 'Fade Out'.

summary

Of course, as you've noticed by now, some level of technical involvement is inevitable, but believe me, the true secret is to know the essentials of the software and to have a clear idea of the style, feel and sound of the music you want to record. And remember, the great thing about Cubase is that, for the most part, you can choose how deeply into the technical details you wish to go, how much comprehension of various functionality you require for your own individual needs and how much techie-specie you might need to garner from the program's comprehensive manuals. But in the meantime, try your hand at another studio session and see if you can make some further improvements to your recordings.

chapter 7

studio session 3: organising a project

By now you've probably begun to discover that, when it comes to organising a recording session and laying down tracks in Cubase SX, there's always a number of ways of doing the same job. Because Cubase SX is so packed with features and functionality, it's easy to become overwhelmed by the sheer potential on offer. However, as I've said before and will probably say again, think about the style of music you're trying to record and the overall sound you're trying to achieve, then think about how you like to work. Do you like to adjust every possible parameter manually, or are you happy to automate certain tasks and features? Do you want to play every real instrument yourself, or are you happy to use samples or MIDI instruments? Are you recording set songs with arranged parts, or do you want to use Cubase as part of the creative process of composing and arranging 'on the fly'? How complicated are your arrangements and instrumentation? What are the limitations of your overall system? Cubase SX is like a powerful graphic application such as like Photoshop or even Quark XPress – everyone uses it differently and few use absolutely everything.

As you've seen, it's reasonably straightforward to select an audio or MIDI track, press the Record button and end up with a track to work with, but as you come to use Cubase SX more and more, you might find that you want a bit more visual feedback to help you get a fuller picture of what's going on with your song at each stage in the recording and polishing process. For instance, depending on the size of your monitor, you'll probably want to keep the Project window and the Inspector open during recording, and you'll always want access to the Transport panel. You may also want to keep the VST Channel Mixer open to monitor the level of your input signal during recording. (Incidentally, when you start recording seriously, it always pays to save all of the files related to a particular song in the same folder so that, when you need to find them at a later date, you won't have to go searching all over your hard disk.)

OK, so now you know the basics of audio and MIDI recording and you can

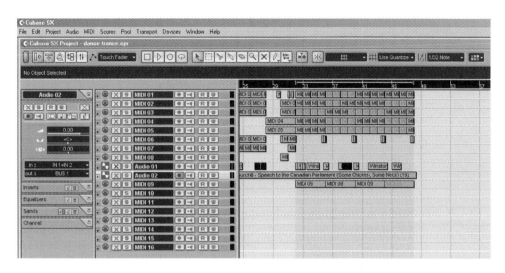

Tracks and MIDI events in the Project window

record tracks into Cubase. You know what tools to use for basic editing functions and you know how to access VST effects and instruments, and you also know about the internal mixers and how you might begin to mix and process the tracks you've recorded. Now it's time to get back into the virtual studio and have a look at some of these features in more detail. While you're there, you can check out some other techniques and functionality that might improve your creative working practices and help you polish that final mix.

monitoring the situation

The term *monitoring* generally refers to listening to the input signal during recording, and this is an important aspect of any session. Essentially, you have a choice of three options: you can monitor via Cubase SX itself, externally by listening to the signal before it reaches Cubase SX or by using ASIO Direct Monitoring, which is a combination of both of these methods. If you choose to monitor via Cubase SX, the input signal is mixed in with the audio playback. The advantage here is that you can adjust the monitoring level and panning in the Mixer and add effects and EQ to the monitor signal, just as you would during playback. The disadvantage of monitoring via Cubase SX is that the monitored signal will be delayed by latency, the value of which will depend on your particular audio hardware and drivers. What this means is that efficient monitoring via Cubase SX requires an audio-hardware configuration with a low latency value. When monitoring via

Cubase SX, you can select one of four modes in the Preferences dialog of the VST page. These modes include:

- **Manual** – Allows you to turn input monitoring on or off by clicking the Monitor button in the Track list or in the Mixer

- **While Record Enabled** – Allows you to hear the audio source connected to the channel input whenever the track is record enabled.

- **While Record Running** – Switches to input monitoring only during recording

- **Tape Machine Style** – As the name implies, this emulates standard tape-machine behaviour by input monitoring in Stop mode and during recording, although not during playback.

External monitoring – listening to your input signal before it goes into Cubase SX – requires some sort of external mixer so that the audio playback can be mixed with the input signal. This can be a stand-alone physical mixer or a mixer application for your audio hardware, as long as your virtual mixer has a mode which allows the input audio to be sent back out again (usually called something like 'Thru mode' or 'Direct Thru mode'). The disadvantage of monitoring externally is that you can't control the level of the monitor signal from within Cubase SX or add VST effects or EQ to the monitor signal. However, the advantage is that the latency value of the audio-hardware configuration doesn't affect the monitor signal in this mode. If you do want to use external monitoring, you need to make sure that monitoring via Cubase SX isn't activated as well, so disable this simply by selecting the 'Manual' monitoring mode in the Preferences dialog of the VST page and, well, don't activate the Monitor buttons.

If you're using ASIO 2.0-compatible audio hardware, it will probably support ASIO Direct Monitoring. In this mode, the actual monitoring is done in the audio hardware itself by sending the input signal back out again. However, monitoring is still effectively controlled from Cubase SX, which means that the audio hardware's Direct Monitoring feature can be turned on or off automatically by Cubase SX, just as it is when you're monitoring internally. To activate ASIO Direct Monitoring, open the 'Device Setup' dialog box on the Devices menu and use the 'Direct Monitoring' checkbox on the 'Setup' tab for the VST Multitrack device. If the checkbox is greyed out, forget it – your audio hardware, or perhaps its current driver, doesn't support ASIO Direct Monitoring. If you have any questions about this, contact your audio hardware's manufacturer.

When ASIO Direct Monitoring is activated, you can select a monitoring mode in the Preferences dialog of the VST page, just as you would if monitoring in Cubase SX. Depending on the nature of your audio hardware, it may also be possible to adjust monitoring levels and panning from the Mixer. However, VST effects and EQ cannot be applied to the monitor signal in this mode, since the monitor signal doesn't actually pass through Cubase SX. Again, depending on your audio hardware, there may be special restrictions concerning which audio outputs can be used for direct monitoring. Fortunately, when Direct Monitoring is activated, the latency value of the audio-hardware configuration doesn't affect the monitor signal.

take two

Although a single audio track can play back only one audio event at a time, an extremely useful function in Cubase SX allows you to record a number of 'takes' on one track. This means that you can either keep going until you get just the right take of a particular vocal or instrumental track, or you can cut and paste sections from various takes to make a perfect take that you can then use in the rest of your mix. For example, by using Cycle Record mode set to 'Create Events', you'll create one continuous audio file encapsulating the entire recording process. For each recorded lap of the cycle, one audio event will be created and the events will have the name of the audio file followed by the word 'take' and a number indicating the number of the take. Your last take will end up on top and will be the one you hear when you activate playback.

If you want to listen to any of your other takes, just select another take for playback by right-clicking the event and selecting 'To Front' from the pop-up menu that appears. You'll also see another submenu listing all of the other events. When you select the take you want, the corresponding event is brought to the front, and this is a particularly useful feature in that it allows you to combine the best parts of each take quickly by using the Scissors tool to split the events in several sections, one for each part of the take. Since the original take events overlap each other, clicking with the Scissors tool will split all takes at the same position, and you can use the 'To Front' function to bring the best part of each take to the front. This allows you to combine the best sections of each take quickly, using the first line from one take, the second line from another take and so on to compile a perfect – or, at least, the best possible – take in the Audio Part Editor.

a bit more audio

As I mentioned in Chapter 4, 'Studio Session 1: Laying Down Tracks', when you record something in Cubase SX, an audio file is created on the hard disk and an audio clip is created in the Project window, with the latter referring to the former. However, an audio event is also created in Cubase SX, and this is what plays back the audio clip. Believe it or not, there are good reasons for this. The audio event is the object that you place on a time position in Cubase SX. If you make copies of an audio event and move them to different positions in the project, they'll still all refer to the same audio clip. Furthermore, each audio event has an Offset value and a Length value. These determine the positions in the clip at which the event will start and end, ie which section of the audio clip will be played back by the audio event. For example, if you resize the audio event, you'll change just its start and/or end position; the clip itself won't be affected.

The audio clip doesn't necessarily refer to just one original recorded file. For example, if you apply some processing to a section of an audio clip, this will actually create a new audio file that contains only the section in question. The processing will then be applied to the new audio file only, leaving the original audio file unchanged. Finally, the audio clip is automatically adjusted so that it refers both to the original file and to the new, processed file. During playback, the program will switch between the original file and the processed file at the correct positions, but you'll hear this as a single recording with processing applied to just one section. This feature makes it possible to undo processing at a later stage and apply different processing to different audio clips that refer to the same original file.

As you should also know by now, for an audio event to be played back in Cubase SX, it has to be placed on an audio track. This is similar to a track on a multitrack tape recorder, but in Cubase you can view the event and move it along the Timeline to another position. You can place any number of audio events on an audio track, but only one can be played back at a time. Also, you can have a virtually unlimited number of audio tracks, although the number of tracks you can play back at the same time depends on your computer's performance.

Even though audio events can be placed directly on audio tracks, sometimes it's convenient to gather several audio events into an audio part. This is simply a container allowing you to move and duplicate several audio events as one. From this point on, each audio track has a corresponding audio channel in the Mixer - much like a channel on a hardware mixer - allowing you to set levels and add things like panning, EQ and effects.

back to the fold(er tracks)

As the name implies, a folder track is a folder that...well, that contains a number of other tracks. Moving tracks into a folder provides a useful way of structuring and organising groups of tracks in the Project window - for example, grouping several tracks in a folder track makes it possible for you to hide tracks and give yourself a lot more working space on the screen, also making it quicker and easier to solo and mute several tracks and edit several tracks as a single entity. They can contain any type of track, including other folder tracks.

Folder tracks can be used in many helpful ways, but a good way of grasping their potential is by considering how your arrangement breaks down, in terms of sections. For example, if you're composing an orchestral piece, you might decide that all of the various string sounds you're using - violins, violas, cellos etc - can be regarded as a section - that is, as a single mixable entity. If you create a folder track called, say, 'Strings' and place all of the associated channels inside it, not only can you temporarily hide them within the Project window but you can also reduce the number of (temporarily) visible channels in the Track Mixer merely by closing the folder. (If you're using a lot of instruments, the Track Mixer can end up being wider than even two 21" monitors can display at once.) It also means that, as long as you've mixed the components of the folder relative to one another, you can then close the folder and use only the fader for the 'Strings' folder track within the Track Mixer to control them all at once.

Folder tracks are created just like any other track. Simply select 'Add Track' from the Project menu and then select 'Folder' from the submenu that appears. Once created, you can move any type of track into a folder by dragging and dropping. For example, in the Track list, click on a track that you want to move into a folder and drag it onto a folder track. When the track is placed in the folder track, all parts and events on the track will be represented by a corresponding folder part that displays a graphic representation of all parts and events in the folder. Since you can move any type of track into a folder track, it's possible to create subfolders by moving one folder track into another. This is called *nesting*, and it allows you to have, say, a folder containing all of the vocals in a project, and each vocal part could have a nested folder containing all of the takes you're using in a subfolder for easier handling. You can hide or show the tracks located in a folder by clicking on the Show/Hide button (the + sign) in the Track list for the folder track. Remember, hidden tracks are still played back as usual, and when a folder is closed the folder parts still give you a graphic representation of the parts and events within the folder.

A particular advantage of using folder tracks is that they provide you with a convenient way of muting and soloing several tracks as a single unit. Muting and soloing a folder track affects all tracks in a folder, although you can also solo or mute individual tracks in the folder. Like all other tracks, to mute a folder track (and thereby all tracks within it), simply click the Mute (X) button in the Track list. Folder tracks can be muted in much the same way, but by clicking the Solo button instead. To solo or mute tracks within a folder, show the tracks in the folder and use the Mute and Solo buttons in the Track list as usual for any tracks inside the folder.

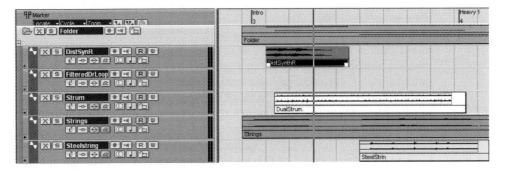

Folder track showing the tracks contained within

As you can partially see in the illustration above, the parts contained in a folder track are shown as folder parts, and a graphic representation of the contained events and parts are shown with horizontal/vertical position and length position in the Track list, just like in the Event display. If part colours are used, these are also shown in the folder part.

When several tracks have been put into a folder track, the parts and events on the tracks may end up in several separate folder parts. A new folder part is created automatically if there is a gap between parts and events on the tracks or, in certain circumstances, if there is an overlap between the folder part and an event on a track within the folder. Within folders, you can perform most standard editing commands like cut, copy, paste and move; the only difference compared to normal part or event editing is that all tracks in the folder are affected.

multitrack recording

Among all of the cool features introduced in Cubase VST, there was a function called 'multi-record', which always seemed like a bit of a mystery to dedicated non-manual readers, although it did become a popular subject for Steinberg Technical Support. In a way, Cubase SX has retained this feature and, depending on the sort of music you record, there are occasions when using multi-record, or 'Multiple', will make your life a lot easier.

So what exactly can you do with 'Multitrack' or 'Multiple' recording? Well, to begin with, these functions allow you to record a group of performers all at the same time and still have their performances appear on one track each. This can be particularly useful if the audio channels you're about to record aren't related directly but you still want to record them at the same time. If you have a keyboard or some other MIDI controller that can transmit on several MIDI channels, you can record different MIDI channels onto different tracks.

As you should already know by now, to add a track to a Project, simply select 'Add Track' from the Project menu and select a track type from the submenu that appears. A new track will be added below the currently selected track in the Track list, and of course the Add Track menu is also available as a separate item on the Quick menu. For multitrack recording, there is an additional option at the bottom of the Add Track submenu called 'Multiple'. When you select this option, it brings up a dialog box allowing you to add more than one track in one operation. You can decide whether audio, MIDI or group tracks should be created by selecting the relevant number in the 'Count' value field, located in the pop-up menu within the dialog box.

quantizing

In music perhaps more than anything else, timing is everything. Without it, your whole composition and performance falls apart. That's why one of the most used features in Cubase, no matter what style or genre of music you play, is the Quantize function. Although I looked at this function briefly in earlier sessions, it's definitely worth getting to know more about it on an intimate basis.

Cubase SX offers a number of different types of quantize functionality, but in principle quantising is simply a function that automatically moves recorded notes to exact note values. If, for example, you record a series of eighth notes, some of them may end up slightly beside the exact eighth-note positions, and quantizing the notes to eighth notes will move the 'misplaced' notes to exact positions. But of course quantising is more than merely a method of correcting errors; it can also be used creatively in a variety of ways and doesn't always have to be used or applied to your entire piece. For example, the 'quantize grid' doesn't have to consist of perfectly straight notes, and if required some notes can automatically be excluded from Cubase's Quantize function. And when you quantize MIDI, only the notes are affected, not any other event types. You can also quantize audio events, and this is a very useful function if you're producing dance music, particularly if you're working with loop splicing.

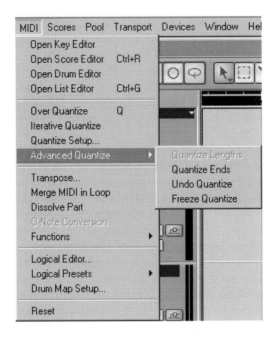

Quantize options in Cubase SX

At its most basic, setting up quantizing involves selecting a note value from the Quantize pop-up menu on the toolbar in the Project window or a MIDI Editor. By default, this allows you to quantize to exact note values only, so if you want more options you'll have to select 'Quantize Setup' from the MIDI menu or 'Setup' from the Quantize pop-up menu, which opens the 'Quantize Setup' dialog box, shown at the top of the next page. Any settings made in the dialog are immediately reflected in the Quantize pop-up menus.

The three quantising types you'll probably use most in Cubase SX are Over Quantize, Iterative Quantize and Groove Quantize. Like I said, with MIDI parts, quantizing affects only the notes and leaves other kinds of MIDI messages unchanged. Apart from Iterative, your original notes will always be used for calculating any subsequent quantizing, since none of your MIDI data is changed permanently.

Here's a brief look at each type of quantize:

- **Over Quantize** – This is the one you'll probably use the most, since it's the Cubase equivalent of a spellcheck or auto-correct. Over Quantize moves your notes to the closest quantize value without changing the

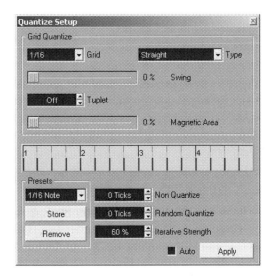

The 'Quantize Setup' dialog box

actual lengths of the notes themselves. It also detects if your playing is consistently behind or ahead of the beat and will quantize your chords in a reasonably intelligent manner.

• **Iterative Quantize** – This is a good choice if you want to clean up your timing but don't want a feel that's too rigid or precise. Instead of moving a note to the closest quantize value, this option moves it only part of the way, allowing you to specify how far the notes should be moved towards the selected quantize value. As only notes further away than the specified value get moved, you can allow for a certain amount of loose timing while still being able to tighten up those really dodgy notes. Specify how much the notes should be moved towards the grid with the 'Iterative Strength' setting in the 'Quantize Setup' dialog box.

Iterative Quantize is also different from regular quantization in that the operation is not based on the notes' original positions but on their current, quantized positions. This makes it possible to use Iterative Quantize repeatedly, gradually moving the notes closer to the quantize grid until you achieve the desired timing.

• **Groove Quantize** – As the name implies, this option is used to create a rhythmic 'feel' or 'groove' rather than simply to correct errors. With the Groove Quantize setting, Cubase compares your music with a groove pattern and moves notes so that their timings match that particular groove. This feature has improved slightly since Cubase VST, allowing you either to create your own rhythmic templates or groove maps or to use the selection of grooves included in Cubase SX.

Generally, you just need to remember that quantizing affects only MIDI notes, not other event types, and that any quantizing carried out in the Project window applies to all selected parts, affecting all notes within them. In the Key Editor, too, quantizing applies to all selected notes – if no notes are selected, all notes will be affected.

hitpoints, audio slices and groove extraction

Hitpoint detection is a special feature of the Cubase SX Sample Editor and is used for tempo-related operations, automatically detecting attack transients in an audio file and then adding a type of marker, or *hitpoint*, at each transient. These hitpoints allow you to create *slices*, where each slice ideally represents each individual sound or beat in a loop. (You'll probably find that drum or other rhythmic loops work best with this feature.) When you've successfully sliced an audio file, you can:

- Change tempo without affecting pitch

- Extract timing or a groove map from a drum loop and then use this to quantize other events to the same settings

- Replace individual sounds in a drum loop

- Edit the actual playing in a drum loop without affecting the basic feel

- Extract sounds from loops

Incidentally, the term 'loop' in this context means an audio file with a musical timebase. For example, the length of the loop represents a certain number of bars and/or beats at a certain tempo. Playing back the loop at the right tempo in a cycle set to the correct length will produce a continuous loop without gaps.

generating hitpoints

To generate hitpoints, start by importing your sample into the Pool. You can also use part of an audio track, but if you do, be careful; you're best off doing a bounce on the area you want to work on, as the sliced part will replace the original sample in all instances that use it. If you do a bounce, it's best to use a slightly larger area so that you can snap the loop later on.

Now open this sample/bounce in the Sample Editor and switch to the hitpoint layer. Depending on your material, you might already have good hitpoints, and you can check this easily with the Speaker tool – just click on the area between two hitpoints and the resulting slice will be played. If you're not satisfied with your hitpoints, try the sensitivity slider; most hitpoints sound OK at one level of sensitivity, but there are often some missing at vital points which appear if you increase the sensitivity value – but only after other, useless hitpoints are created. Depending on the ratio of useless to useful hitpoints, either crank up the sensitivity until the missing hitpoints appear and use the Lock tool to fix them in place and reduce sensitivity again or use the Disable tool to click off the useless hitpoints.

Unfortunately, some points never appear, no matter what sensitivity setting you use, but in this case you can manually add the missing hitpoints with the Pencil tool. If you find that the hitpoints are generated slightly too late – a few milliseconds, say – check your source material. This mostly happens with material that was created with samplers where the event starts with noise or just a DC offset. If this is the case, you should use the Move tool to relocate the hitpoints to better positions. If your hitpoints are randomly placed all over the sample, not just at the right places, your sample probably contains a lot of different sounds and/or melodies. To fix this, select the right loop and filter the hitpoints via the Use function so that only rhythmically placed ones are used. (You'll probably need to use the Disable tool to disable/enable some hitpoints in order to adjust to swing, for example, or you might even need to draw in or move some additional hitpoints.)

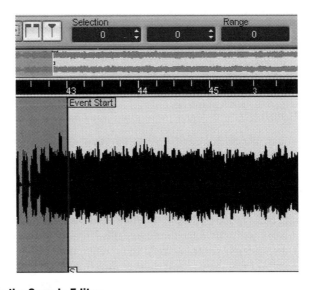

Inserting hitpoints in the Sample Editor

You'll often find that you have to use combinations of the above techniques, so just play around a little until you get the hang of things. Don't worry if you make a mistake – everything you do is in the Undo History.

adjusting loops

At this point, you'll probably have to adjust your loop if you don't have a one-bar sample already cut correctly. You'll need to do this now because the selection will automatically snap to hitpoints and, if desired, to zero-crossing points. To go about doing this, hit the Loop button in the toolbar, play the sample and, while it's playing, make and adjust your selection. When you hear the loop you want, hit [P] on your keyboard or select 'Loop Selection' from the Transport submenu in the Context menu. Now you should adjust the number of bars and beats in your selection, as well as its signature, after which the original tempo of your source audio is displayed right next to your selection. Another method is to adjust the loop pointers directly; if your ruler shows bars and beats (ie the default setting), you can compare them to your hitpoints and see if the loop fits.

The basic idea of using hitpoints to slice up a loop is to make a loop fit the tempo of a song, or alternatively to create a situation that allows the song tempo to be changed whilst retaining the timing of a rhythmic audio loop, just like using MIDI. Audio file types that will give the best results when sliced using hitpoints include those where each individual sound in the loop has some kind of noticeable attack; things like slow attacks and legato playing might not produce the desired result. You'll also definitely find that poorly recorded audio might be difficult to slice correctly, and 'normalizing' a file first will improve Cubase's performance in this respect. There may also be problems with sounds that are drowned in a 'smearing' effect, such as short delays.

using hitpoints

To make use of hitpoints, start by creating your slices by selecting the Hitpoints submenu from the Context menu and then selecting 'Create Slices'. Now drag your selected sample onto an audio track and it will be adapted to the song tempo. If the sample is already being used in the arrangement, all instances will be replaced and you can open this part and move, copy, mute or delete slices or split the sliced part in the arrangement and work with the slices individually. If you change the tempo, the slices will stay at their rhythmic positions, while if you hear an annoying clicking, enable 'Autofades' to remedy the situation. To do this, open the Inspector for the track in question and click on the Autofades icon or use the Context menu in the Track list to enable all fades. Depending on the change in speed you require, you'll need to select either a fade-in or -out or a crossfade. Select a time between 1ms and 10ms to apply fast fade-ins and slow fade-outs respectively.

When your song tempo is fixed and you've deleted all of the slices you don't want (ie you've muted/unmuted slices until you're sure you don't want them), you can time-stretch the slices by selecting 'Close Gaps' from the Audio submenu in the Context menu. (Don't worry, if you change your mind later on, you can undo this.) Afterwards, you can disable Autofades without hearing a resulting click.

using groove templates

To create and use Groove Templates, again go to the Context menu and the Hitpoints submenu, then select 'Create Groove Quantize' to create the groove template. Only one bar can be used; if you have multibar patterns you have to create several grooves, each with one bar selected as the loop. As I mentioned earlier, you can choose this groove in the Quantize menu if you want to draw notes by hand. However, with the Curve Draw functions, don't use the Length Quantize function (linked to the Quantize function), as this just presets the curve form.

You can also open the quantize set-up, choose your groove (and save it) and use it to quantize your MIDI or audio events. However, if you just want to quantize a take, you don't need to loop it – just generate and correct the hitpoints, letting your take stay in the arrangement without bouncing it, and in the arrangement select 'Divide Audio Events' from the Hitpoints submenu in the Context menu. Now you can move and quantize directly.

summary

Hitpoints have been greeted with a mixed response by users of previous versions of Cubase. While it's possible, and indeed easy, to use hitpoints in the Audio Editor for slicing up audio to change the tempo of a loop, it's not possible to use hitpoints in the Tempo Track Editor in Cubase SX as it was with Cubase VST's Mastertrack Editor. Previously, you were able to add metre- and time-based hitpoints and link them together in pairs, while you also had the option of straightening up the linking lines – Cubase would automatically work out the tempo changes required to make certain time-based events fall on a certain beat. This used to be extremely useful for transcribing MIDI recordings if you didn't play them to a metronome, and for many it's frustrating that Cubase SX doesn't work this way. But these complaints come mostly from producers working in video, so it won't be of much concern to most home users. For now, let's carry on with our studio sessions and take a look at some more useful functions for enhancing your musical mix.

chapter 8

studio session 4: mixing

While a lot of people, particularly musicians, focus on the recordings themselves, much of the creativity and personal satisfaction of the entire music-creation process can often come in the mixing session. In many respects, mixing is where all the hard decisions get made, and the work done at this stage can make the difference between a workmanlike recording and a masterpiece of sound, even starting with the same source material. And when you finish your mix, you'll need to think about mastering your mix to a medium like DAT or CD. This takes some special skill, but it's also something you pick up with experience.

Before the modern era of multitrack tape and the eventual evolution of desktop digital studios, recording and mixing were essentially part of the same process. You had to get a good balance between the voices and instruments and the best possible sound right there at the session because there was no way of making radical adjustments later. In these situations, the final recording simply needed to sound as close to the original as possible. Although that still might be your personal final goal, with Cubase SX you have a lot more flexibility in how you lay down your tracks and how you ultimately mix those tracks to create your own personal sound. When you record, basic monitoring facilities can provide you with a reasonable 'ear' for adjusting a range of things such as level, pan and auxiliary sends. And since with Cubase you'll hear exactly what's on your tracks as you progress through the recording, if your monitor mix sounds good, you can be reasonably sure that your final mix will sound great. That's why you should always regard everything you do as being part of the finished product and make it as perfect as possible.

mixing in Cubase SX

Ideally, as a musician working with Cubase SX, you'll probably want to start the mixing process as soon as your project gets off the ground. While you should have a pretty clear idea of the sound you're aiming for, always allow a certain amount of scope for creativity and synchronicity, depending on the nature and style of your song; if you're working on a dance record, for instance, you need to understand the style well enough to know the elements of the music that your audience demands and should always look for new and different sounds and textures to add to those elements to push your particular style that little bit further.

One of the great advantages of recording with Cubase SX is that you're in control. You're the one that knows how every step of the preparation and recording process is going to contribute to the final mix. This means that, without the interference of an extraneous engineer or producer, the mixing stage should in theory be straightforward and painless. In practice, however, what this really means is that, among other things, you're totally responsible for getting the arrangement right and selecting the right sounds, making sure the musicians are playing in time and in tune and obtaining a good performance from the singer by whatever means necessary. If there's a problem in any of these areas, you can turn a deaf ear to it only for so long – and that's about as long as it takes you to get to the mix. Any problems present in your tracks at the mixing stage will have to be disguised, covered up or fixed, if possible. But as I mentioned earlier, because of the power and functionality of Cubase, you should be thinking about fixing things as you go along, and if there's a problem with a performance or with the way in which a particular track is recorded, those problems should be corrected as soon as they occur. Remember, this is *your* studio and *you're* the one that has to play producer and engineer as well as, perhaps, writer, performer and arranger.

setting up a mix

A fairly traditional style of album recording involves putting down all of the basic tracks, overdubbing other instruments and vocals and then taking a break for a few days before starting to mix the whole lot. The main disadvantage of working a song at a time, all the way from laying down basic tracks to mixing, is that your ears go woolly after a while and you can easily lose perspective and artistic judgement. Over-familiarity with your song and the recording could mean that you won't be able to judge it in the same way as a punter would. Taking a break between recording and mixing means that you can come back to the song with fresh ears and hear very clearly which bits need to be brought out and which elements play an important but, perhaps, subservient role.

Mixing is fairly straightforward, but making a good mix is a bit trickier. Since you may not be a sound engineer, using Cubase SX as a musician means that you don't need to know all of the technical details of how to mix. But as a musician, you do need to be able to recognise when something is right and be able to understand what's missing when it isn't.

It's important to keep in mind the purpose of your mix. Is it a dancefloor mix that should sound great on a club PA, or is it intended for CD listening at home? Depending on your style and approach, you might even want to create a radio mix, emphasising some sort of 'buy me' factor – whatever you think that might be – that will attract particular listeners to your release. Just don't think that Cubase SX will guarantee you a place on *Fame Academy* or make you the next Pop Idol. And personally, I'd consider that a big plus.

formats

Once you've done your mix, you'll probably want to transfer it to DAT or burn it onto a CD. Audio geeks and sound-tech junkies still whinge that DAT isn't always entirely satisfactory because it reproduces only 16-bit sound, which means that its sound quality isn't any better than the CDs people listen to at home. Personally, I tend not to worry about things that I can't hear. Most of the work that I've done in traditional studios has been dumped to DAT, and the CD masters produced from them haven't been noticeably inferior in any way, shape or form to anything else out there. And despite earlier warnings about using MiniDiscs, in a lot of cases they will also work just fine.

With the range of modern CD burners and various plug-ins and audio software available, it's possible to record, mix and even master a complete album with Cubase SX. I know that for a fact because I've done it myself and have produced a CD which is selling quite well at the moment. Once you've got a CD master, you can either flog it around to commercial record companies or you can send it off to any number of CD producers, who will be able to press and package any number you like at very competitive prices.

But let's not get too far ahead of ourselves. Cubase SX still has a lot of functionality that you might find useful during both the recording and mixing stages, so first have a crack at this final studio session and see what else you can do.

channel settings

The Channel Settings window in the Mixer is used for adding effects and EQ to individual audio channels. Each audio channel has its own Channel Settings window, and when using the 'Extended Channel Strip' viewing option the upper panel can be set to show different views for each audio-channel strip. Select what to display for each channel by using the View Options pop-up menu at the top of each channel strip.

Channel settings are used to apply EQ, send effects and insert effects and to copy complete channel settings and apply them to other channels. In each case, all channel settings are applied to both sides of a stereo channel. Use the Initialise Channel button at the bottom of the Channel Settings Common panel to reset a channel to the default setting. Default settings in Cubase SX are as follows:

• All EQ, insert and send effect settings are deactivated and reset

• Solo/mute is deactivated

• The fader is set to 0dB

• Pan is set to the centre position

**EQ section of the Channel Settings window
with four modules activated**

Each EQ module contains a fully parametric one-band equaliser with the following parameters:

• **Gain** - Governs the amount of boost or attenuation around the set frequency. The range is +/-24dB.

• **Frequency** - The centre frequency for the equalisation. Around this frequency, the sound will be boosted or attenuated according to the Gain setting. The range is 20Hz-20kHz.

- **Q** - Determines the width of the frequency band to be affected around the centre frequency. The narrower the frequency band, the more drastic the effect of boost or attenuation. For the leftmost and rightmost EQ modules, the following special modes are available:

1 If the Q value for the leftmost EQ module is set to minimum, it will act as a low shelving filter

2 If the Q value for the leftmost EQ module is set to maximum, it will act as a high-pass filter

3 If the Q value for the rightmost EQ module is set to minimum, it will act as a high shelving filter

4 If the Q value for the rightmost EQ module is set to maximum, it will act as a low-pass filter

more on EQ

As any producer will tell you, EQ can make or break a mix. Just as a painter will mix primary colours to accentuate certain areas of a painting and draw the eye across the canvas, so too the producer will mix high, low and mid-range frequencies to achieve subtle colourings of tone that any good mix demands. When you listen back to one of your mixes, two or more sounds operating in the same frequency can often combine in synergy to create a new sound that is greater than the sum of its parts. This blending of sound creates new timbres as well as forcing sounds apart, and the separation of sounds is particularly important in most dance music as a lot of low frequencies infringe on each other's wavelength - for example, bass lines and kick drums. Similarly, a lot of jungle producers will pitch up their drum loops to allow low basses to sit comfortably in the mix. The same applies to mid-range sounds - snares, hi-hats and bongos all tend to occupy a similar wavelength and will need to stand out from each other.

EQ can vastly affect the character of a sound, but if it's used subtly the presence of a sound can be changed without its tonal quality being affected, and this is the key to creating the spacious mixes we're all familiar with. And just as it is with effects, with EQ less is more, so always try to cut frequencies before you have a go at boosting them.

Although some people insist on adding EQ while recording, as a general rule it's best not to. One good reason for this is that, when you create a mix and find out that it's not what you were hoping for, you can go back to a blank sound canvas by resetting your EQ levels and starting again. Another reason is that there's no way you can really know what EQ a sound finally needs until you hear it in context with the rest of a mix, and trying to EQ an already EQ'd sound can create some ugly noises. Remember, some sounds in your mix will have to take a back seat and won't be heard on their own, so why record them with heavy EQ as if they were up-front solos?

frequencies

As a musician, you may or may not be interested in delving into a lot of techie detail, but when it comes to EQ it's definitely worth knowing a little about frequency settings for particular instruments. This will at least give you an idea of where to start with your EQ settings in Cubase, although you don't have to worry too much about whether or not you actually understand the science. To begin with, an instrument's sound is made up of a fundamental frequency, the musical note itself and harmonics, even when only a single note is played, and it's these harmonics that give the note its unique character. If you use EQ to boost the fundamental frequency, you simply make the instrument louder and don't bring it out in the mix. You should also note that a particular frequency – 440Hz, say – corresponds directly to a musical note on the scale (which, in the case of 440Hz, is the A above middle C, hence the tuning reference 'A-440'). Boosting the harmonic frequencies, on the other hand, boosts the instrument's tonal qualities and can therefore provide it with its own space in the mix. Below are some useful frequencies for various instruments:

- **Voice** – Presence, 5kHz; sibilance, 7.5-10kHz; boominess, 200-240kHz; fullness, 120Hz

- **Electric Guitar** – Fullness, 240Hz; bite, 2.5kHz; air/sizzle, 8kHz

- **Bass Guitar** – Bottom, 60-80Hz; attack, 700Hz-1kHz; string noise, 2.5kHz

- **Snare Drum** – Fatness, 240Hz; crispness, 5kHz

- **Kick Drum** – Bottom, 60-80Hz; slap, 4kHz

- **Hi-Hat And Cymbals** – Sizzle, 7.5-10kHz; clank, 200Hz

- **Toms** – Attack, 5kHz; fullness, 120-240Hz

- **Acoustic Guitar** – Harshness/bite, 2kHz; boominess, 120-200Hz; cut, 7-10kHz

TIPS

Here are some general tips for getting a better overall sound:

- *Always listen to the whole track dry, with no effects, no EQ, nothing. This will help you determine were things want to sit. Of course, if the song you're mixing utilises processed samples, you won't be able to do this, although a relatively effective way of reducing effects on pre-processed samples is to use a limiter or some form of compression. You can also target the frequency band in which the sample is most effected and reduce the gain, although this can lead to unwanted tonal change.*

- *Thin out pads, backing vocals and acoustic-guitar parts with EQ. Perversely, this dramatises the dynamics rather than diminishing them.*

- *Smoothe the curve. Although not to everyone's taste, this is definitely familiar as the radio-friendly 'pro sound' of most modern records. The polished feel seems to rest in the mid band, with producers tending to cut frequencies between 200Hz and 4kHz, chopping the most in the 600Hz–1kHz region.*

  OK, forget the techie crap. On a graphic equaliser like the one you have in Cubase SX, EQ carried out like this forms a smooth upside-down curve which you can draw in graphically. Professional producers take down the mid range, as middle frequencies have a habit of tiring the ear and blocking the finer frequencies. (This holds especially true on tracks with a profusion of guitar.) The 'edge' that's apparently so desirable is not achieved by boosting the mid range – which seems natural – but by tweaking the top and bottom frequencies so that they interact with contrast.

TrueTape

While digital audio recording has many benefits, some musicians have expressed the opinion that digital sound always tends to be somewhat sterile and cold when compared to high-quality analogue recordings, and indeed, a few years ago, Neil Young was particularly outspoken about the evils of digital sound. However, TrueTape claims to remedy this problem by recreating that good old 'open-fire' sound of analogue tape saturation at the recording stage. TrueTape was first introduced in Cubase VST version 5, offering a unique Steinberg technology that emulates the behaviour of a professional analogue tape recorder. If you're particularly into acoustic music, you might want to play around with this – as long as your system can handle it.

TrueTape analogue-tape emulator

TrueTape produces 32-bit *float files*, and all of the hard-disk and processor-speed considerations of the regular 32-bit format apply here. Unlike the regular 32-bit mode, however, you can make use of the TrueTape mode even if your audio hardware only supports 16-bit resolution, because the TrueTape feature converts the signal to 32-bit float format and adds audio information in the floating-point domain.

To begin, simply pull down the Devices menu and select 'TrueTape', using the Drive control to adjust the amount of tape saturation effect to your liking. If you're monitoring through Cubase SX, you'll hear how the changes colour the sound of the monitored signal, allowing you to try out the settings before actually recording. There's a pop-up menu above the TrueTape panel that allows you to select one of four Drive presets if you want to effect quick changes. These contain no hidden parameters, so selecting the '24dB Super Saturation' preset is the same as moving the Drive control all the way to the right. (Note that any adjustments you make to the Drive control are automatically applied to the selected preset.) You can also rename a preset by double-clicking and typing in a new name. Raising the Drive level will also raise the level in the audio file and will allow you to reach 0.0dB clipping on the input-level meters easily. However, unlike when recording in 16-bit format, this is nothing to worry about; Steinberg say that it's virtually impossible to get digital distortion in a 32-bit float file.

pods and pans

As I mentioned briefly earlier on, when you're mixing, you've got to decide where in the mix you want each of your instruments, vocals or other sounds to be positioned. This involves panning sounds and instruments to appropriate positions in the stereo mix in order to achieve the desired level of depth and texture. Although panning can be used quite creatively, as a general rule vocals, bass drum, bass instruments and often snare drum are usually panned to the centre. (In some types of music, though, you might want to pan the snare slightly off-centre.) Vocals can also be panned a little to the left or right, but they tend to sound better if there's a balancing vocal or similar instrument panned to the opposite side. Other instruments, like guitars, brass, keyboards and backing vocals, can be panned to either side. And remember to pan stereo effects like reverb fully left and right if your want to create width in your mix. Of course, you can pan any instrument, vocal or pad sound back and forth in your mix, depending on the effect and degree of movement you're trying to achieve.

You should be aware that, in the Project Setup dialog box, there's a pop-up menu named 'Stereo Pan Law', and from this you can select one of three pan modes. This is all related to the arcane fact that, without power compensation, the power of the sum of the left and right sides will be higher (ie louder) if a channel is panned to the centre than if it's panned to the left or right. To remedy this, the Stereo Pan Law setting allows you to attenuate signals panned to the centre by -6dB or -3dB (the default setting). Selecting the 0dB option effectively turns off 'Constant-Power Panning'. Experiment with the modes to see which fits best in a given situation.

TIPS

- *Don't rely on the pan controls to keep your sounds separate; try to get your mix working in mono first and then start panning the various elements. After you get a rough balance in mono using no EQ, you can then start to play around with the fine tuning.*

- *When you're actually recording, try to make your up-front sounds slightly brighter while keeping background and supporting sounds less bright. Since it's always easier to cut frequencies using EQ than to add them later, just make sure you've got enough top end in your various recordings.*

- *To keep that contrast in your mix, don't process everything. If you do, you'll just end up with a muddy cacophony of competing sounds, or something that sounds vaguely like hip-hop.*

pods

As studios become more compact, solutions for instrument recording follow suit. At present, manufacturers offer a competitive range of amp-modelling hardware and software that simulates the 'genuine' sounds of an amp, including effects. This means that you don't have to mic up any hardware and also means huge savings in terms of space and money.

The current favourite models are those in the Pod series created by Line6. A guitar and a bass Pod can be had for around £200 ($315) each, and each unit offers pre- and post-EQ effects, serious EQ and a preset range of classic amp models. It's also possible for you to create your own patterns and models, which means that the classic Marshall valve you've always wanted can be created with a few tweaks. Even someone who thinks 'mike' is a good wholesome Christian name will get a sound that engineers train for years to achieve.

An alternative to the Pod system can be found in the J-Station, manufactured by Johnson Amplification. This gives guitar and bass modelling along with acoustic-guitar simulation. Both systems are fully programmable.

automation

For all the idlers out there, it's probably comforting to know that virtually every mixer and effect parameter in Cubase SX can be automated. You can do this either by manually drawing curves on automation subtracks in the Project window or by using the Write/Read functions and adjusting parameters in the Mixer itself. There's no real difference between the two techniques in terms of how the automation data is applied; the methods differ only in the way in which the automation events are created, either by being manually drawn in or recorded. Any applied automation data will be reflected in the Mixer, by a moving fader and a corresponding automation track curve. In Cubase SX, you can completely automate your mix, and the following parameter settings can be recorded automatically or drawn in manually on automation subtracks.

Essentially, in Cubase SX, there are three types of automation tracks available: channel-automation tracks, plug-in automation tracks and a master automation track. There is one automation track for every audio, group and MIDI track, and also one for each activated ReWire and VST instrument channel. This automation track has a number of automation subtracks, one for each channel setting available, and each channel's insert-effect program selection and effect-parameter setting is handled by the channel automation track. For MIDI tracks, all track parameters, MIDI send and insert-effect parameter settings are also handled by the channel-automation track.

There's one plug-in automation track for each automated send and master effect and one for each automated VST instrument. These tracks have a number of automation subtracks, one for each parameter of each automated effect and VST instrument.

For each project, there's only one master automation track, and this track can have any number of automation subtracks, just like a single audio track. The

Master Gain parameter controls all of the bus-output levels and the send effects' 'master' input levels. In Cubase SX, automation subtracks are not separate tracks but rather separate 'views' of the same automation track, showing one automation parameter at a time.

For each audio and group track you can automate the following:

• Volume

• Pan left to right

• Pan front to rear

• Mute

• EQ Master Bypass

• FX Send Bypass

• Settings for four EQ modules (Enable, Freq, Quality and Gain)

• Eight effect-send On/Off switches

• Eight effect-send levels

• Eight effect-send Pre/Post switches

• Surround-pan parameters (if used)

• Eight insert-effect program selection and effect parameters (if insert effects are used)

Meanwhile, from the master automation track, you can automate the following parameters:

• Master gain

• Left and right levels for all output buses

• Send effects 'master' input levels

If audio effects are used, for each plug-in automation track you can automate the following:

- Send-effect program selection and effect parameters

- Master-effect program selection and effect parameters

- VST instrument program selection and parameters

(Keep in mind that there is one plug-in automation track for each automated send effect, master effect and VST instrument.)

For each MIDI track you can also automate:

- Volume

- Pan

- Mute

- Track parameters On/Off switch

- Transpose

- Velocity shift

- Random 1-2 Min/Max/Target

- Range 1-2 Min/Max/Target

- Four insert-effect On/Off switches

- Four send-effect On/Off switches

- Four MIDI insert-effect parameters (if used)

- Four MIDI send-effect parameters (if used)

TIP

When you're editing automation data in the Controller Editor, it's possible to display two or more channels simply by shift-clicking on them in the panel on the left-hand side. If you're working with stereo or group channels, for instance, you'll need to shift-click in order to display both the left and right channels. Using the Crosshairs and Pencil tools, you can draw automation data in all displayed channels simultaneously by holding down [Ctrl] + [Alt].

VST System Link

VST System Link is a new feature in Cubase SX that provides a network system for digital audio that allows you to have several computers working together in one large system. Unlike conventional networks, it doesn't require a boring plethora of Ethernet cards, hubs or CAT-5 cables; instead, it uses the kind of digital-audio hardware and cables you probably already have kicking around your studio. VST System Link has been designed to be simple to set up and operate while still providing enormous flexibility and performance gains in use. It's capable of linking computers in a ring network, where the System Link signal is passed from one machine to the next, eventually returning to the first machine, and the networking signal can be sent over any type of digital-audio cable, including S/PDIF, ADAT, TDIF and AES, as long as each computer in the system is equipped with a suitable ASIO-compatible audio interface.

So why, you may ask, would you want to link up two or more computers? Well, the added computer power this would give you could open vast vistas of possibilities. For example, you could dedicate one computer to running VST instruments while recording audio tracks on another. If you happened to need lots of audio tracks, you might simply add tracks on another computer. Or you could have one computer serving as a virtual effects rack, running nothing but processor-intensive send-effect plug-ins. And since you can use VST System Link to connect different VST System Link applications on different platforms, you can take advantage of effect plug-ins and VST instruments that are specific to certain programs or platforms.

To use VST System Link, you'll need at least two or more computers. Because Cubase SX is clever, these can be of the same type or use different operating systems. This means you can link an Intel-based PC to an Apple Macintosh without problems, as long as each computer has audio hardware with specific ASIO drivers installed and working. The audio hardware must also have digital inputs and outputs and, of course, in order to be able to connect up the computers, their digital connections must be compatible. You'll need at least one digital-audio cable for each computer in the network and the VST System Link host application installed on each computer.

At the time of writing, VST System Link is implemented for Cubase SX, Nuendo 1.6 and Cubase 5.1 (System Link version), and any VST System Link applications can connect to each other. On top of that, Steinberg recommend that you use a KVM (Keyboard, Video, Mouse) switchbox.

OK, so what's a KVM switchbox? Well, if you want to set up a multi-computer network, or even a small network in a limited space, it's a good idea to invest in one of these switchers, which allow you to use the same keyboard, monitor and mouse to control each computer in the system and switch between computers very rapidly. KVM switchers aren't too expensive and are very easy to set up and operate. It you decide not to go this route, the network will function just the same, but you might end up doing a lot of jumping from one machine to the other while setting up.

and then...

There are a few more things to keep in mind at all times during the mixing phase of your project, and if I'm repeating myself here then it's probably because it's important (although a touch of early senility isn't out of the question).

To begin with, don't mix at a constantly high volume. For that matter, don't constantly mix at the same volume. Check your mix frequently using a very low volume and at various mid-level volumes, and every now and then crank it up to really hear how things hit hard. Look at your speakers when you do this to make sure you're not overdriving them.

When the mix is finished, you should listen to it from start to finish at a high level, turning the volume down again if you need to make further alterations. Your ears can get tired, woolly and even damaged if you listen to loud music for long periods, causing you to hear a muffled version of the sound that you're listening to. OK, maybe that sounds like your parents blathering on about the evils of rock music, but believe me, you don't want to mess with your ears. If you're a musician, you need to keep them in the best possible condition.

Finally, a well-arranged and well-tracked song shouldn't require a great deal of fader-riding. You might have to bring up a lead instrument here and there, but that should be about it.

chapter 9

plug-ins and VST instruments

VST is now the most common native audio plug-in and was actually pioneered by Steinberg, the manufacturer of Cubase SX. With a format that avoids platform incompatibility, VST plug-ins are available in both PC and Mac versions and provide help in handling all of the usual studio effects such as compression, limiting, gating, reverb, echo, chorus and flanging, and there's also an increasing range of plug-ins coming onstream for things like pitch correction, applying creative or gratuitous distortion, vocoding, denoising, click suppression, spectral enhancement and other such esoteric functions. As is common with conventional mixers, effects such as reverb and echo can be used in an effects-send-and-return loop on the virtual mixer so that a single plug-in can be applied to as many channels as needed without soaking up exceptional amounts of processing power. However, other plug-ins, such as compressors or equalisers, still have to be used on a per-channel basis and must be patched in via controls in much the same way as you would patch them in on a traditional console.

Cubase SX continues to build on the collection of plug-ins that Steinberg licensed to third-party developers in VST version 5.1, with a little help from a new blue interface and a few notable additions. Newly bundled plug-ins that were previously sold separately include the useful DeEsser from SPL and Craig Anderton's funky QuadraFuzz. In the VST instrument cupboard, SX has kept most of the plug-ins from 5.1 but has wisely chosen to ditch the dodgy-sounding Universal Sound Module for General MIDI. For versatility at producing bass, pad, poly lead and effects patches, Steinberg has added a new virtual analogue synth called A1, developed by Waldorf. Since SX seems to have finally overcome the latency problems that dogged earlier versions of Cubase, all of these VST instruments now seem to perform faultlessly. Well, nearly faultlessly.

VST instruments

As you've probably gathered, VST instruments are software synthesisers or other sound sources that can be contained within Cubase SX. They're played internally via MIDI and their audio outputs appear on separate channels in the Mixer, allowing you to add effects or EQ just as you can with other audio tracks. While a reasonable assortment of VST instruments are included with Cubase SX, a growing number of others can be purchased separately from Steinberg and other manufacturers.

While the limitation of eight send effects and eight master effects found in earlier versions of Cubase is still in place, SX now allows you to run a maximum of 32 VST instruments simultaneously, depending on the capacity of your processor. Since most VST instruments are multitimbral and have multiple outlets, using all of the possible virtual instrument channels available to you would be downright silly, even if you could find a PC powerful enough to run them all. Some VST MIDI windows such as the Arpeggiator and IPS have been left out of SX as well, but in exchange you've now got an open-ended MIDI plug-in architecture at your disposal with which you can format other plug-ins.

VST instruments can be accessed from the Devices menu, and the default 'rack' that appears can contain up to 32 VST instruments. However, the maximum number of instruments depends on your computer's performance and the complexity of the instruments selected. VST instruments that are now bundled with Cubase SX include:

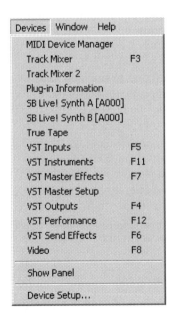

Selecting VST instruments from the Devices menu

- CS40

- JX 16

- LM-9

- Neon

- LM-7, a reasonable 24-bit drum machine that has up to 12 voices, compared with LM-9's nine voices, and receives MIDI in Omni mode (ie on all MIDI channels). When you're using it, you don't need to select a MIDI channel to direct MIDI to LM-7, and the unit responds to MIDI Note On and Note Off messages. The plug-in comes with six sets of drum sounds, with 'Compressor', '909' and 'Percussion' loaded as the default sounds, while 'Modulation', 'Fusion' and 'DrumNbass' can be loaded by selecting the Load Bank command from the File menu and opening the file named 'lm7_second_set.fxb', which you'll find located in the 'Drums' subfolder of the folder named 'VSTplugins'. Compressor features samples of an acoustic drum kit, 909 features classic analogue drum-machine sounds and Percussion, as it says on the tin, features various percussion sounds.

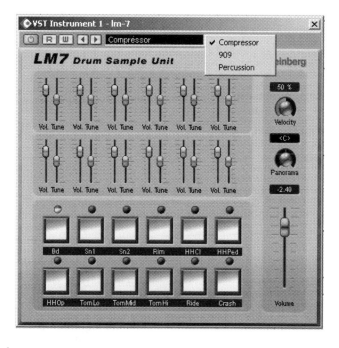

LM7 VST synth plug-in

- A1, a particularly good dual-oscillator software synthesiser originally developed by and licensed from Waldorf. The A1 is essentially a polyphonic synth unit with up to 16 voices, multimode filters including low-pass, bandpass, high-pass and notch filters and PWM (Pulse Width Modulation). The unit also includes FM (Frequency Modulation), a ring modulator and a built-in stereo chorus/flanger effect. A1 receives MIDI in Omni mode, on all MIDI channels, so you won't need to select a MIDI channel to direct MIDI to the unit. And, of course, the unit responds to MIDI controller messages.

  The keyboard shows incoming MIDI note data as if played by invisible hands and can be 'played' by clicking on it with the mouse. However, if you're playing it in this way, the velocity produced will be fixed and you won't actually be able to record anything.

A1 VST synth plug-in

- VB1, a reasonably mediocre virtual bass instrument built on somebody's idea of real-time physical-modelling principles.

  OK, it's not got the class of a 1962 pre-CBS Fender Jazz bass, but VB1, which has had a slightly different-coloured face-lift since appearing in Cubase version 5, still sort of looks like a fairly funky virtual bass. VB1 is polyphonic, able to play up to four voices and receives MIDI in Omni mode (ie on all MIDI channels). As on a 'proper' electric bass, the Volume control regulates the volume and the Damper switch controls the length of time that the string vibrates after being plucked. You can adjust the position of the pick-

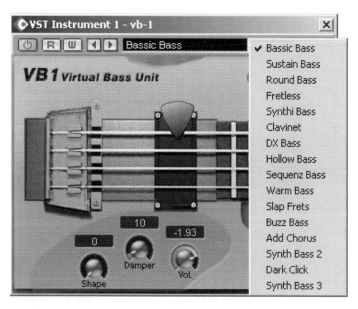

VB1 virtual bass VST plug-in

up and by dragging the 'mic' left or right, thus changing the tone; positioning it towards the bridge position produces a hollow sound that emphasises the upper harmonics of the plucked string while moving it towards the neck position makes the tone fuller and warmer.

Meanwhile, the 'pick' position determines the point along the length of the string where the initial pluck is made and controls the roundness of the tone, just as the pick does when playing a real guitar. The Wave Morph function selects the basic waveform used to drive the plucked string model, and be aware that this parameter can drastically change the character of the sound produced; the control smoothly morphs through the waves, so if you're not careful you might end up creating sounds that have no relation to a bass guitar. Then again, there might be times when you'd want to do that.

All things considered, the bass sounds from the VB1 aren't all that wonderful, and with this plug-in it's probably a case of 'nice interface, pity about the sound'. You'll probably get a better bass sound out of Neon (or this might just be my own personal taste).

To access a VST instrument, open the Devices menu and select an unused MIDI track in the Project window. Pull down the Output pop-up menu for the

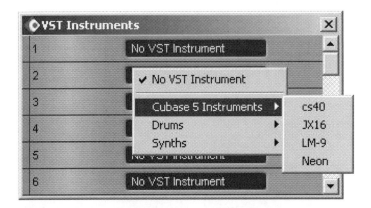

**Selecting Cubase 5 instruments (top), drums (middle)
and synths (bottom) in Cubase SX**

MIDI track in the Track list or in the Inspector. The pop-up menu will now contain an additional item with the name of the activated VST instrument. Once you've done this, choose your desired VST instrument in the MIDI Output pop-up menu. The output from the track will then be routed to the selected instrument. Depending on the selected instrument, you may also need to select a MIDI channel for the track.

TIP

Latency is a term that describes the length of time it takes for a MIDI instrument to produce a sound when you press a key on your MIDI controller, and it can be a problem with VST instruments. For instance, depending on your audio hardware and its ASIO driver, the latency value may simply be too high to allow comfortable real-time VST instrument playback from your keyboard. However, one way around this problem is to play and record your parts with another MIDI sound source selected and then switch to the VST instrument for playback.

drums

Drum sounds are assigned to note values on your MIDI keyboard, as listed below. All mapping is GM-compatible.

DRUM SOUND	NOTE VALUE	COMMENT
Bass	C1	
Rim	C#1	Compressor only
Snare	D1	
Clap	D#1	909 only
Hi-Hat	F#1	
Open Hi-Hat	A#1	
Tom 1	A1	
Tom 2	B2	
Tom 3	D2	
Crash	C#2	
Ride	D#2	Compressor only
Tambourine	F#2	Percussion only
Cowbell	G#2	Percussion only
Hi Bongo	C3	Percussion only
Lo Bongo	C3#	Percussion only
Conga Mute	D3	Percussion only
Conga Open	D#3	Percussion only
Conga Lo	E3	Percussion only
Timbale Lo	G3	Percussion only
Timbale Hi	G#3	Percussion only
Cabasa	A3	Percussion only

VST effects

Cubase SX also boasts a range of new - or, at least, newly licensed - VST effects bundled for your producing pleasure. These include plug-ins such as DeEsser, Reverb A, Step File and the ubiquitous Vocoder.

DeEsser

A de-esser is used to reduce excessive sibilance, primarily on vocal recordings, so that your singer doesn't end up sounding like Gollum drooling on and on about his preciousssssss. Essentially, a de-esser is a special type of compressor that's tuned to be sensitive to the frequencies produced by the 's' sound, hence the name. Close-proximity microphone placement, pop shields and EQ can help you get the overall sound just right, but depending on the diction of your vocalist, you could still end up with a problem with sibilance. Conventional compression and/or equalising may not easily solve this problem, but a de-esser can.

SPL DeEsser VST plug-in

Reverb A

Reverberation is often used to add ambience and a sense of space to recordings and is probably one of the most important and most commonly used effects in popular and vocal-driven music. Reverb A is a Cubase SX reverb plug-in which provides your recordings with smooth, dense reverb effects. Although this product is new to the PC, a similar plug-in called Reverb 32 did appear in the previous Mac version of Cubase, VST/32. You can get some particularly nice effects on both vocals and instrumentals with this new plug-in, but keep in mind that reverb, like all effects, should be used sparingly.

Reverb A VST plug-in

StepFilter

StepFilter provides you with a pattern-controlled multimode filter that can create rhythmic, pulsating filter effects and produce two simultaneous 16-step patterns for the filter cut-off and resonance parameters, synchronised to the tempo of the sequencer. You can set step values manually by clicking in the pattern-grid windows, and individual step entries can be freely dragged up or down the vertical axis or directly set by clicking in an empty grid box. By click-dragging left or right, consecutive step entries will be set to the pointer position. The higher up the vertical axis a step value is entered, the higher the relative filter cut-off frequency or filter resonance setting. When you start to play back and edit the patterns for the cut-off and resonance parameters of the filter, you can hear precisely how your patterns affect the sound source connected to StepFilter directly.

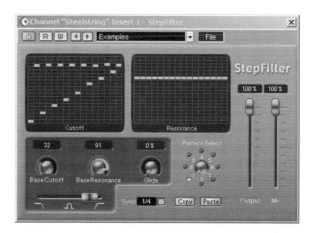

StepFilter VST plug-in

Vocoder

Through the rather dubious experimentation that went on in the world of '80s pop, most of us now know all too well what a vocoder is. The question is, do we have the good sense not to use it? A vocoder works by applying sound or voice characteristics taken from one signal source, called the *modulator*, and applying them to another source, called the *carrier*. A typical application of a vocoder is to use a voice as a modulator and an instrument as a carrier, making the instrument 'talk'. A vocoder works by dividing the source signal (the modulator) into a number of frequency bands so that the audio attributes of these individual frequency bands can be used to modulate the carrier.

In Cubase SX, the Vocoder plug-in has a built-in carrier which is basically a simple polyphonic synthesiser, although if you really have to, you can also use an external carrier. In MIDI mode, the Vocoder is set up slightly differently from the other plug-ins because this sort of set-up requires both an audio signal (as the modulator source) and a MIDI input (to play the carrier) in order for the effect to work properly. Generally, the modulator source can be audio material from any audio track, or even a live audio input routed to an audio track. Make sure you have a low latency audio card installed before trying this at home.

A good source of modulator material can include talking or singing voices or percussive sounds such as, say, drum loops. Static pads or soft ambient material don't work all that well for use as modulators, but if you don't mind producing something atrocious, there are no absolute rules governing what can or can't be used as a modulator source.

Vocoder VST plug-in

QuadraFuzz

Craig Anderton's funky QuadraFuzz plug-in is now included in the Cubase SX set of VST effects, providing a high-quality distortion effect. This plug-in allows you a degree of control over level divided into four frequency bands, both before and after distortion. With such a high level of control, you can create a very wide selection of distortion effects, ranging from the sublime to the ridiculous. The main window features four Filterbank controls, the Master Gain and Output controls and a preset selector. In the editor window, which is opened by clicking the Edit button in the bottom-right-hand corner, you can access a Frequency Band display in which you can set the width of the frequency bands as well as their levels before distortion.

QuadraFuzz VST plug-in

accessing VST effects

In Cubase SX, you can apply up to eight different insert effects per channel, and you'll find that most effect plug-ins will work flawlessly as insert effects. In general, the only restrictions are with the number of inputs and outputs in the effects, and for a plug-in to be usable as an insert effect it has to have one or two inputs and one or two outputs. The number of inputs and outputs will be determined by whether the insert effects are being used on a single mono audio channel or on a stereo channel pair. If you're using stereo audio channels, you'll need to use an effect with stereo inputs. While it's possible to use a mono-input effect with a stereo-channel pair, only the left channel in the pair will be processed, which probably wouldn't be the sort of thing you'd want. For mono audio channels, you can use mono or stereo input effects, but since the audio channel is in mono, the output of the effect will also be in mono. For stereo-output effects, the left channel will be used.

Routing an audio channel through insert effects is fairly simple, since insert-effect settings are available in the Mixer in Extended mode, the Channel Settings window and the Inspector. As an example, if you bring up the Channel Settings window, you'll notice that the inserts are located to the right of the channel strip. Pull down the Effect Type pop-up menu for one of the insert slots and select an effect. If you hold down [Ctrl] while selecting an insert effect, this effect will also be selected in the same insert slot for all Mixer channels.

Now, to make sure that the effect is activated, check to see that the On button for the insert slot is lit. If necessary, open the effect's control panel by clicking the Edit button and use the Mix parameter to adjust the balance between dry and effected signal. When one or several insert effects are activated for a channel, the Insert Effects buttons light up in blue on the Mixer and Track list. Click on the button for a channel to bypass all of its inserts, which will turn the button yellow. To turn off an effect completely, pull down the Effect Type pop-up menu and select 'No Effect'. It's always a good idea to keep this setting for all effects that you don't intend to use in order to minimise unnecessary processor load.

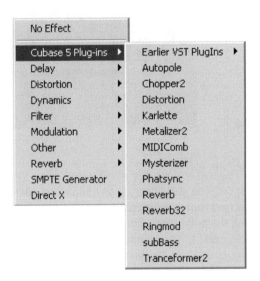

Selecting VST effect plug-ins
in Cubase SX

There are also eight master effect slots available in a separate window or from the Master section in the extended Mixer. When you select and activate master effects, either select the Extended mode for the Mixer and show the Master section or pull down the Devices menu and select 'VST Master Effects' to bring up the Master Effect window, then pull down the pop-up menu for one of the master-effect slots and select an effect. To change the settings of the effect, click the Edit button to bring up its control panel and similarly, as described above, to turn off a master effect select 'No Effect' for the corresponding slot. Note that master-effect plug-ins must be at least stereo in/out, so if you find you have a plug-in in your 'VSTplugins' folder that you can't assign as a master effect, the reason is probably that it's a mono plug-in.

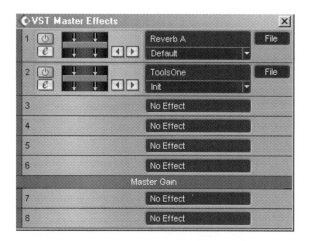

The 'VST Master Effects' dialog box

accessing VST instruments

Earlier, I mentioned briefly how to access VST instruments, but to fully activate and play them you'll need to pull down the Devices menu and select 'VST Instruments' from the VST Instruments panel which appears, complete with 32 slots. Next, pull down the pop-up menu for an empty slot in the panel and select your desired instrument. You'll then need to select an unused MIDI track in the Project window and pull down the Output pop-up menu for the MIDI track in the Track list or in the Inspector. This menu will now contain an additional item with the name of the activated VST instrument. Select the VST instrument on the MIDI Output pop-up menu and the MIDI output from the track will be routed to the selected instrument.

Depending on the selected instrument, you may also need to select a MIDI channel for the track, so always check the instrument's documentation for details on its MIDI implementation. Now make sure that 'MIDI Thru Active' is activated in the Preferences dialog and click on the Monitor button for the MIDI track in the Track list, Inspector or Mixer. When this is activated, or when the track is record enabled, incoming MIDI is passed on to the selected MIDI Output, which in this case is the VST instrument.

Now, if you open the Mixer, you'll find an additional channel strip for the instrument's audio outputs. Notice that VST instrument channel strips have the same features and functionality as group-channel strips, with the addition of an Edit (e) button at the top of the strip for opening the VST Instrument control panel. You can use the pop-ups at the bottom of the channel strips to route the instrument audio to the desired output or group and then, *voilà*, you can play the instrument from your MIDI keyboard. You can now also use the Mixer settings to adjust the sound, add EQ or effects, etc, just as with regular audio channels. Of course, you can also record or manually create MIDI parts that play back sounds from the VST instrument if you want to. A word of warning, though: while Cubase SX allows you to have up to 32 VST instruments activated at the same time, software synthesisers can consume quite a lot of processor power, so it's always a good idea to keep an eye on the VST Performance window to avoid running out of steam at a crucial moment.

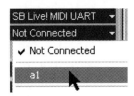

Selecting VST instruments from the VST Instruments dialog box (above) and the Project window (below)

TIP

While everyone agrees that Cubase SX is now a great deal better at automatically compensating for latency when plug-ins are used as insert effects on audio tracks, this is still not necessarily true for group channels, VST instrument channels or ReWire channels. With this in mind, you should use the VST Dynamics plug-in only as an insert effect for audio-track channels, and possibly as a master effect, if you're using only a single stereo-output bus.

additional plug-ins

Apart from the new and newly licensed set of plug-ins featured in Cubase SX, in order to ensure compatibility with songs created in previous versions of Cubase, Steinberg has included most of the previous standard set of VST plug-ins. These include old favourites with colourful names such as Chorus, Phaser, Overdrive, Chopper, Metalizer and Grungelizer, while also included is the more prosaically named but extremely useful Dynamics.

Chorus

This adds a short delay to the signal and pitch-modulates the delayed signal to produce a doubling effect. It's often a nice effect to be used on acoustic instruments, particularly guitars and strings, or for rounding out pad sounds. If you don't overdo it, chorus can create an illusion of movement and help you build a front-to-back perspective in the mix. However, it does detune your sound a bit, and it can also get a bit samey if it's too strong and can push sounds further back in a mix.

Phaser

Unlike the classic *Star Trek* weapon that can be set to stun or kill, the Phaser plug-in produces the classic swooshing sound immortalised in stunning iconic rock tracks such as The Small Faces' 'Itchycoo Park' and Status Quo's nearly credible 'Pictures Of Matchstick Men'. (Just kidding about the 'stunning' and 'iconic', by the way.) Of course, this effect has been used in many different ways by many different artists. It works by shifting the phase of a signal and adding the result back to the original signal, causing partial cancellation of the frequency spectrum. It's very good for pads, but it can muddy a mix if over-used. Use it effectively in combination with other effects.

Overdrive

Overdrive is a distortion-type effect that emulates the sound of a guitar amplifier. There's a selection of factory styles available and none of these are stored parameter settings but different basic overdrive algorithms. Like Distortion, the characteristics of the styles found on the Overdrive plug-in are indicated by their names, and this effect could be helpful if you wanted to sound like the late great Jerry Garcia or the even later and greater Jimi Hendrix.

Chopper

With no connection whatsoever to a Harley Davidson or Easy Rider, Chopper2 is an effect that uses different waveforms to modulate the level (tremolo) or left-right stereo position (pan) of a signal, either using the Tempo Sync facility or manual modulation-speed settings. It can be used to produce tremolo-style effects and can also produce autopan effects when set to stereo. It livens up synth sounds and works well with a flanger.

Metalizer

The Metalizer plug-in feeds an audio signal through a variable-frequency filter, applying Tempo Sync or time modulation and feedback control. If you're a fan of Ozzie and the crew, this is great if you're looking for that Aerosmith or Black Sabbath sound.

Grungelizer

The Grungelizer adds noise and static to your recordings, producing sounds that sound like those produced by an old radio with bad reception or a worn and scratched vinyl record. It's great for use with beats, samples and for remixes, or for artificially ageing a sound, and it can also be used with other effects to create an absolutely filthy guitar sound.

VST Dynamics

You can radically alter the dynamic range or level of audio material in Cubase SX with the built-in dynamic processor. Each audio channel has its own 'VST Dynamics' section, and this panel gives you access to AutoGate, AutoLevel, Compress, SoftClip and Limit processors. When you click on one or more of the processor label buttons, the dynamic is inserted after any regular insert effects and before the EQ section and channel fader.

So what do these weird processor names actually do? Well, compared to plain vanilla dynamics, VST Dynamics has two additional modules called AutoLevel and SoftClip. The signal flow is fixed, in the order AutoGate-AutoLevel-Compress-SoftClip-Limit. Be aware that VST Dynamics has a higher inherent latency than regular effects, so signals will be delayed when passing through the plug-in. Here's a run-down of the processors' functions:

- **AutoGate** - A noise gate similar to hardware devices found in traditional studios and used for cutting out unwanted signals like noise and interference which may be present between sections wanted material.

- **AutoLevel** - An automatic level control designed to even out signal differences in audio material and to boost low-level signals or attenuate high-level signals.

- **Compress** - Like the standard audio compressors used in traditional studios, this converts loud parts into quieter parts and quiet parts into louder parts.

- **SoftClip** - This is like an automatic gain control which you can't really adjust. It's designed to keep sounds within certain decibel parameters and create a warmer, valve-amp-style sound.

- **Limit** – This performs the same role as a hardware limiter and is generally used to stop an output signal from passing above a set threshold, no matter how loud the input becomes.

VST Dynamics panel

summary

VST instruments and plug-ins are being aggressively marketed as convenient, cheap alternatives to the usual range of expensive hardware synths, samplers and rack effects, and for the most part they probably are. However, they still take up a huge amount of memory and will ravenously devour whatever processing power you have available. Plug-in effects normally provide fairly trouble-free performance, although some of them can introduce a slight delay to an audio signal.

That said, VST instruments can save you loads of money on more expensive hardware synths, although they may not be as convenient to use, depending on your style of music and playing. And before you use any effect in your music, it's probably worth asking yourself, 'Why?' – or, perhaps more specifically, 'Is this really necessary?' VST makes effects so easy to use that there's always the temptation to over-use them just because you can. Remember that effects are there to create an illusion, so don't let them become delusions.

chapter 10

what about the Mac?

Ralf Hütter of Kraftwerk once said that you can synthesise your existence. Commenting further on the nature of electronic music, he went on to remind us that the real meaning of the word *synthesis* is 'putting together' and to admit that, essentially, that's all he really did.

In 2002, Apple received the Technical Award at the Grammys, an event that honours individuals and companies who have made contributions of outstanding technical significance to the recording field. Also awarded was Robert Moog, the man whose name is synonymous with the synthesiser. This was a prestigious award for Apple, since recipients of the Technical Grammy Award are determined by the vote of the members of the Recording Academy's Producers' and Engineers' Wing, a group of 5,000 pro-audio professionals dedicated to developing new technologies, recording and mastering standards, as well as other critical issues affecting their craft.

According to the Recording Academy's president, Michael Greene, Apple and Robert Moog's technical and creative innovations, inventiveness and versatility constitute 'towering achievements of true visionaries'. And why not? In a number of respects, the products of their inspiration introduced electronic technology into the public consciousness, put the power of creation in the hands of the individual and more or less revolutionised the entire recording industry.

Despite the best efforts of the Wintel mob to convince musicians and producers that PCs offer a cheaper and equally competent option, Apple is still considered to be the leading architect in bringing computer technology into the studio and revolutionising the way in which music is written, produced, mixed, recorded and creatively imagined. Even in its earliest days, the Mac helped launch a number of important software breakthroughs, linking technology to the creative process and literally changing the face of the recording studio, and over the past decade the Mac has become virtually synonymous with digitally driven production techniques, providing almost anyone with the ability to compose, perform, record, edit and mix a song or even an entire album.

Although the Mac has made it particularly easy to put together music, it has also (probably inadvertently) contributed to the escalating confusion between good sounds and good ideas. And as Brian Eno suggested, because it's so easy to produce music, we sometimes forget to ask why we're producing it. In a perceptive endpiece in *Sound On Sound*, Mark Wheery actually goes as far as to suggest that all this great technology has, for the most part, killed off any good musical ideas and that somewhere, in this delicious digital process, how we record music has become confused with how we write music, which means that, in most popular music, good, creative and original composition has been replaced by - or synthesised with - great production of increasingly mundane, similarly arranged, technology-dependent sounds.

Cubase and the Mac

Falling into the often misleading realms of received-wisdom marketing, Steinberg chose to release the Windows version of Cubase SX first and took its good old time with announcing a public release date for the Mac version. To be fair, this probably wasn't entirely Steinberg's decision, since Cubase SX is designed to run only on Apple's OS X and certain technical issues concerning MIDI and audio functionality weren't properly resolved until Apple finally released a finished version of Jaguar, or OS X 10.2. Steinberg has now stated that, with Apple's release of their newest desktop and laptop systems, the Mac, with its PowerPC G4 processor, is perfectly suited to running high-end, native audio solutions. And with both Cubase SX and Nuendo now running on Mac OS X, music and media production has never been easier or faster.

Cubase SX is now fully optimised for the dual-processor Power Mac G4, taking full advantage of the speed available with the PowerPC G4 processor. For the practising musician, this gives you all the power and unrivalled ease of use to do whatever you want. A dual 1GHz Power Mac G4 provides Cubase SX with more DSP power than the Power Mac G3 computers, giving you the flexibility to really load up on plug-ins for true real-time processing performance. Although I do have to declare an interest here as a life-long Mac-user, it has also been proven in head-to-head tests that, despite the usual fnords, even an 867MHz G4 is 80 per cent faster than a 1.7GHz Pentium 4.

So how, you might ask yourself, can this be? Doesn't clock speed determine how fast a computer actually runs? Well, in a word, no - or, at least, not entirely. Despite the unshakeable belief, perpetuated by Microsoft, Intel and most computer retail outlets, that megahertz equals performance, in reality it's only a contributing factor towards real performance. When you compare chips properly, you need to look at things like the process, the size, the number of pipeline stages and the number of megahertz they're running. Most people automatically assume that, because a Pentium 4 runs at 1.7GHz, it's faster than the 867MHz G4, that the bigger number equals a faster speed. Physically, the G4 is half the size of the hot, fat and sweaty Pentium, which also runs through 20 pipeline stages compared to the G4's seven. And that's where the discrepancy appears.

Think of it like this. Data needs to be fetched, decoded, executed and stored. Processors do this by essentially pouring this stuff down something that resembles either a soda straw or the Alaskan oil pipeline, depending on the machine. The result is that, although the Pentium clocks up 1.7GHz, because it's got 20 pipelines it actually takes longer to move the data through all of these than it takes the compact and bijou G4 through its seven. (In the demo I saw, the presenter had some cute graphics illustrating lumps of data and the cyber equivalent of air bubbles pumping along these different-sized pipes, but I'm sure you get the idea.) And that, boys and girls, mummies and daddies, is why, despite the megahertz gap, the G4 is over 80 per cent faster than the Pentium 4. Let's just repeat that for those asleep in the back: 80 per cent faster. You can bet that, if there was a big enough media campaign to explain this to the world in words of few syllables, Intel would be losing a lot more than 76 per cent of its share price.

In practice, Cubase SX on the Mac does look pretty much like Cubase SX on the PC and includes all of the same functions, such as unlimited undo/redo, offline process history, professional surround functionality and VST System Link, to name a few. Cubase SX also takes full advantage of the power of Mac OS X, with low-latency native multichannel audio and MIDI support, symmetric multiprocessing and protected memory for a truly rock-solid user experience. And there are plenty more good reasons why so many musicians have decided to pair Cubase with a Mac instead of a PC. Both the Mac and Cubase are easy and really logical to use, and with its VST and ASIO interfaces and future support for Mac OS X's Core Audio, Cubase boasts an unrivalled level of flexibility. (Incidentally, bigger and faster really is better; the minimum system requirement for Cubase SX on the Mac is actually a 350MHz G3 with 256k RAM and OS X. Obviously, a G4 is the machine of choice here, but it's interesting to know that, in true Mac tradition, you can still run Cubase SX on some older machines.)

Having brought you such impressive breakthroughs as VST, LTB and ASIO, Steinberg's revolutionary VST System Link standard now brings true connectivity and platform independence to the digital-audio world, whether you're using a Mac or a PC or both. Not only does VST System Link harness the full CPU and disk power of several computers simultaneously, regardless of platform, but it also lets you take your audio projects to new levels of complexity while offering unbelievable flexibility in your working environment.

And how will this benefit Mac users? Well, for a start, it guarantees 100 per cent unlimited power and flexibility when you upgrade to a brand new dual-processor 1GHz Power Mac G4 or Titanium PowerBook G4. With VST System Link, you can use your old PowerBook or even G3 for instruments, or as an effects rack, or as a virtual mixer. The Mixer Station handles audio playback with lots of EQ and dynamics processing, with virtual instruments running on a second machine. On top of that, both audio and virtual synth tracks run together to the third computer for adding effects such as reverb and flangers. So, with the power offered to you by your new Power Mac G4 and Mac OS X, your creativity really is unlimited.

Mac versus Windows

Although we could get into one of those extremely boring platform debates about the relative superiority of either the Mac or the PC, one of the things a lot of people already undisputedly agree on and probably don't need their minds changed about is the simple fact that the Macintosh is a superb platform for music. Unlike PCs, whose audio capability has always relied on plug-in cards, every Mac motherboard has always had audio capability built in as standard. And of all the machines out there, none is better than the current crop of Mac G4s, which is why over 90 per cent of recording studios and a growing number of serious home studios have them instead of PCs. OK, digital sound has generally come a long way since the early analogue synthesisers of the late 1960s, and today most desktop PCs are capable of reproducing CD-quality sound or working in conjunction with a burgeoning range of digital audio and sampling technology, which includes digital hard-disk recorders, digital sampling instruments, digital sample players/synthesisers and audio device controllers. That is, of course, as long as you can manage to get your assorted soundcards and various other add-on gizmos to work properly in the wacky and wonderful world of Wintel.

On the other hand, apart from some of the early Mac PowerBooks, all Macs have 16-bit stereo audio in and out as part of their basic hardware configuration. You can't do that on any PC unless it's got an extra soundcard or some other audio interface. This means that, although media hype has conditioned most people into believing that PCs are generally cheaper than Macs, by the time you've bought all the extras you need to bring them up to Mac standard, you're probably not really saving all that much. As it happens, a complete mid-range G4 system, like an iMac with trendy flat-screen monitor, fat hard drive and ample memory, will cost less than £1,200 ($1,900) and will provide anything from 16 to 24 audio tracks or more, if you get a really fat hard drive. Twenty years ago, you'd have paid more than that for an eight-track tape recorder. This same Mac system allows you to run a number of virtual samplers with your audio software and loads samples in as little time as it takes to change synth patches on dedicated samplers. As an added bonus, the Mac also adds onscreen graphic editing and provides mix automation for your MIDI tracks, all audio tracks and even virtual instruments.

So, whether Uncle Bill likes it or not, when it comes to music, the Mac is still easier to set up and use than any Windows PC and, contrary to public ignorance, really isn't that expensive. Today's Macs, including the latest flat-screen iMacs, are still the easiest computers to use and easily have more punch for music and digital audio than ever before. Sequencers and plug-ins are expanding to exploit all this power to the full, and if you're using a G4, or whatever comes after, audio latency will be less of a problem and, generally, matching suitable audio cards will be much less hassle. If you don't want to be desk-bound, the latest crop of PowerBooks and iBooks are more than capable of providing excellent mobile-studio facilities for bands on the run.

As far as using Cubase SX is concerned, the program itself is superb on both platforms, and because of the care Steinberg have taken in making the interface and usability consistent, there's probably little in it in terms of sheer performance. However, as a musician, it's up to you to decide which environment feels more comfortable and which system makes it easiest to do what you want to do with your music.

road maps

To paraphrase Douglas Adams' quote about the universe in *The Hitchhiker's Guide To The Galaxy*, Cubase SX is big, mind-bogglingly big, and any book attempting to provide a quick start for practising musicians will never be able to cover every function in minute detail. So, to help plug a few gaps and provide a few pointers on where to look for more information if you happen to decide you need to explore any particular tool or function in more detail, here's a potted synopsis of most of the essential main-menu items to be found lurking in the depths of Cubase SX. You'll find more detailed information on all of these in the .pdf documentation that comes with Cubase SX, and it's also worth browsing the various Cubase- and Steinberg-related websites for updates, tips and fixes. Also, keep in mind that practically every feature in Cubase SX can be customised to look, feel and work the way you want it to, so don't be afraid to experiment.

File menu
New Project

This item allows you to create a new untitled project. A list appears allowing you to select an empty project or a project template and these factory templates are pre-configured to suit various types of project. You can save a project as a template and it will then appear on this list. After making a selection, a 'Project File' dialog box will appear, allowing you to specify the folder in which all files relating to the new project will be stored. Select an existing folder or click the Create button to create a new folder.

Open

This opens a File dialog box allowing you to locate and open saved project files (with the extension .cpr). Several projects can be open at the same time, but only one can be active. The active project is indicated by the red light at the top-left-hand corner of the Project window.

Close

This closes the active window. If the Project window is active, the corresponding project will close.

Save

This saves any changes made to the project since you last saved. The Save command stores the project under its current name and location.

Save As...

This allows you to specify a new name and a new folder for your project.

Save Project To New Folder

This command allows you to save the project into a new empty folder. It has some additional features that can be used for archiving purposes, and when a new empty folder has been selected a dialog appears in which you can change the name of the project and also set the following options:

- Choose to 'Minimise Audio Files', which will crop files based on the audio clips referenced in the project. As the clips used in the project may be references to much larger audio files, this can reduce the size of your project significantly.

- Apply 'Freeze Edits', which will make all processing and applied effects permanent for clips.

- Remove all unused files when you save a project to a new folder. If this is selected, all files relating to the project based on the options set will be saved in the new project folder. The contents of the original project folder will be left untouched. If you're absolutely certain that you don't have any further need for the original project files, you can delete them.

Save As Template

You can save any project as a template so that, when you create a new project, you can base it on the selected template. Saved templates will contain everything that was in the original project, including clips and events.

Revert

This command allows you revert to the last-saved version of a project. If any new audio files have been recorded since you last saved, you have the option of keeping or deleting them.

Import

Audio File

This command lets you import audio files directly into a project, where the imported file will be placed at the current cursor position of your selected audio track.

Audio CD

This opens the 'Import From Audio CD' dialog, where you can import audio from CDs.

Cubase Song/Arrangement/Part

With these functions, you can import songs, arrangements and parts created with previous versions of Cubase (from 3.7 or later). However, due to the complete redesign of Cubase SX, there are certain limitations. Check Steinberg's documentation for details.

MIDI File

With this command, you can import Standard MIDI Files of Type 0 (all data on single track) or Type 1 (data on several tracks). You can choose to import the file into the current project or to create a new project.

Export

MIDI File

As you would expect, this allows you to export your MIDI files as a Standard MIDI Files.

Audio Mixdown

This allows you to export all of your audio tracks, complete with effects and automation, to one or several audio files and in one of several file formats.

Preferences

The Preferences dialog box contains various settings and options and several pages of options. Use the Apply button to make settings without closing the box. There's also a Help button for more information about the items on the selected page.

Key Commands

This dialog allows you to create key commands for virtually any Cubase SX function as well as customise existing key commands to your liking.

Recent Projects

This submenu provides shortcuts to the most recent projects you've been working with. The list is chronological, with the most recent project at the top.

Edit menu

Undo/Redo

Cubase SX offers wide-ranging multiple undo, allowing you to cancel virtually any action you perform. For example:

- To undo the last performed action, select 'Undo' from the Edit menu, or use the corresponding key command (by default [Ctrl] + [Z]). If you select Undo again, the previously performed action will be undone, and so on.

- To redo the last undone action, select 'Redo' from the Edit menu or use the corresponding key command (by default [Ctrl] + [Shift] + [Z]). Undone actions will be available for redo until you perform another action. You can specify how many levels of undo should be available with the 'Maximum Undo' setting on the User Interface page in the Preferences dialog box, opened via the File menu.

History

The Edit History window contains a graphic representation of the 'undo stack' of performed actions, with the most recent action at the top of the stack, and the 'redo stack' or undone actions, with the most recently undone action at the bottom of the stack. The two stacks are separated by a divider line, and the Edit History dialog allows you to undo or redo several actions in one go by moving the divider between the undo stack and the redo stack (in essence, by moving actions from the undo stack to the redo stack, and vice versa).

Cut, Copy and Paste

Like most applications, you can cut or copy selected events (or selection ranges) and paste them in again at the current cursor position on the original tracks.

Paste At Origin

This will paste an event to its original position (ie where it was originally cut or copied from).

Delete

This will delete all selected events.

Split At Cursor

This splits selected events at the currently selected cursor position. If no events are selected, all events on all tracks intersected by the cursor position will be split.

Split Loop

This splits all events at the left and right locator positions.

Range

The items on the Range submenu have the following functions:

Cut Time

Cuts out the selection range and moves it to the clipboard. Events to the right of the removed range are moved to the left to fill in the gap.

Delete Time

The selection range is removed and events to the right are moved to the left to close up the gap.

Paste Time

Pastes the clipboard data at the start position and track of the current selection. Existing events are moved to make room for the pasted data.

Paste Time At Origin

Pastes the clipboard data back at its original position. Existing events are moved to make room for the pasted data.

Split

Splits any events or parts that are intersected by the selection range at the positions of the selection range's edges.

Crop

Crops all events or parts that are partially within the selection range - that is, sections outside the selection range are removed. Events that are fully inside or outside the selection range are not affected.

Insert Silence

Inserts empty track space at the start of the selection range. The length of the inserted silence is equal to the length of the selection range, and events to the right of the start of the selection range are moved to the right to make room. Events that are intersected by the start of the selection range are split, and the right section is moved to the right.

Select

The items on this submenu have different functions, depending on whether the regular Arrow event-selection tool or the Range Selection tool is selected.

Event Selection
- **All** - Selects all events in the window.
- **None** - Deselects all events.
- **In Loop** - Selects all events that are partly or wholly between the left and right locators.
- **From Start To Cursor** - Selects all events that begin to the left of the Project cursor.

- **From Cursor To End** – Selects all events that end to the right of the Project cursor.
- **All On Selected Tracks** – Selects all events on the selected track.

Range Selection
- **All** – In the Project window, this makes a selection covering all tracks, from the project start to the end. In the Sample Editor, it selects the whole clip.
- **None** – Removes the current selection range
- **In Loop** – Makes a selection between the left and right locators. In the Project window, the selection will span all tracks.
- **From Start To Cursor** – Makes a selection from the start of the project to the Project cursor.
- **From Cursor To End** – Makes a selection from the Project cursor to the end of the project
- **Select Event** – Available only in the Sample Editor, this selects only the audio that is included in the edited event.

Duplicate/Repeat

Duplicate
Creates a copy of the selected event and places it directly after the original. If several events are selected, all of these are copied as one unit, maintaining the relative distance between the events.

Repeat
If this is selected, a dialog opens allowing you to create a number of copies (regular or shared) of the selected events. This works just like the Duplicate function, except that you can specify the number of copies.

Fill Loop

This creates a number of copies starting at the left locator and ending at the right. The last is automatically shortened to end at the right locator's position.

Move to

The following functions are available from this submenu:

Move To Cursor
Moves the selected event to the Project cursor's position. If there are several selected events on the same track, the first event will start at the cursor and the following will be lined up end-to-start after the first one.

Move To Origin
Moves the selected events to their original positions, ie the positions at which they were originally recorded.

Move To Front/Move To Back

This function doesn't actually change the position of the events but instead moves the selected events to the front or back, respectively. This is useful if you have overlapping events and want to see one that's partially obscured. For audio events, this is an extra-important feature, since only the visible sections of events will be played back. Moving an obscured audio event to the front or moving the obscuring event to the back will allow you to hear the whole event on playback.

Convert To Real Copy

This creates a new version of a clip that can be edited independently and then adds it to the Pool.

Lock/Unlock

If you want to make sure you don't edit or move an event by accident, you can lock selected events. Locking can affect one or any combination of the following properties:

- **Position** – If this is locked, the event cannot be moved.
- **Size** – If this is locked, the event cannot be resized.
- **Other** – If this is locked, all other editing of the event is disabled. This includes adjusting the fades and event volume, processing, etc.

Selecting locked events and choosing 'Unlock' will unlock the events.

Mute/Unmute

You can mute or silence events by clicking on them and then selecting 'Mute'. As you might imagine, you can unmute the selected events by selecting 'Unmute'.

Macros

A macro is a combination of several functions or commands to be performed in one go, and all macros are set up in the Key Commands dialog. If you have created macros, these will be available on the Macros submenu.

Zoom

The following options are available on the Zoom submenu on the Edit menu:

- **Zoom In** – Zooms in one step, centring on the position cursor.
- **Zoom Out** – Zooms out one step, centring on the position cursor.
- **Zoom Full** – Zooms out so that the whole project is visible. 'The whole project' here means the Timeline from the start of the project to the Length value set in the Project Setup dialog box.

- **Zoom To Selection** - Zooms in horizontally so that the current selection fills the screen.
- **Zoom To Event** - Available only in the Sample Editor.
- **Zoom In Vertical** - Zooms in one step vertically.
- **Zoom Out Vertical** - Zooms out one step vertically.
- **Zoom In Tracks** - Zooms in selected tracks one step vertically.
- **Zoom Out Tracks** - Zooms out selected tracks one step vertically.
- **Zoom Tracks Exclusive** - Zooms in vertically on the selected tracks and minimises the height of all other tracks.

Project menu

Add Track

Adds a track of the type selected on the Add Track submenu. Selecting 'Multiple' allows you to add a specified number of tracks of a selected type.

Remove Selected Tracks

Removes all selected tracks and any parts or events on them from the Project window.

Show Used Automation

Opens all used automation subtracks for all tracks.

Hide All Automation

Closes all open automation subtracks.

Pool

Opens the Pool, which contains all clips that belong to a project.

Markers

Opens the Marker window. Markers store positions to facilitate quick navigation to important locations in a project.

Tempo Track

Opens the Tempo Track Editor. For tempo-based tracks, the tempo can follow the Tempo track, which is activated with the Master button on the Transport panel and may contain tempo changes.

Browser

Opens the Project Browser window. This provides a list-based representation of the project along with graphic editing. This allows you to view and edit all events on all tracks by using regular value editing in a list, or by using tools in a graphic display.

Beat Calculator

A tool for calculating the tempo of recorded audio or MIDI material.

Notepad

Opens a standard text notepad, similar to that used by other applications.

Project Setup

Contains general settings for a project.

Auto-Fades Settings

Opens the 'Auto-Fades' dialog box, where you can specify various fade options.

Audio menu

Process

Basically, you apply audio processing by selecting audio data and then selecting a function from the Process submenu.

Envelope

Allows you to apply a volume envelope to the selected audio.

Fade In/Out

Allows you to set fade-ins and fade-outs.

Gain

Allows you to change the gain (level) of selected audio.

Merge Clipboard

Allows you to mix the audio from the clipboard into the audio selected for processing, starting at the beginning of the selection. For this function to be available, you first need to have cut or copied a range of audio in the Sample Editor.

Noise Gate

Scans audio for sections weaker than a specified threshold level and then silences them.

Normalize

Allows you to specify the desired maximum level of the audio. It then analyses the selected audio and finds the current maximum level and will finally subtract the current maximum level from the specified level, raising the gain of the audio by the resulting amount. If the specified maximum level is lower than the current maximum level, the gain will be lowered instead. Normalizing can be used to raise the level of audio that was recorded at too low an input level.

Phase Reverse

Reverses the phase of the selected audio, turning the waveform upside-down.

Pitch Shift

Allows you to change the pitch of audio without affecting its length, if required. It also allows you to create harmonies by specifying several pitches or to apply pitch-shift based on a user-defined envelope curve.

Remove DC Offset

A DC (Direct Current) offset is present when there is too large a DC component in the signal, sometimes visible as the signal not being centred around the 'zero-level axis', and this function removes any DC offset in the selected audio. DC offsets don't affect what you actually hear, but they affect zero-crossing detection and certain processing, and it's recommended that you remove them. It's also recommended that this function is applied to complete audio clips, since the DC offset (if any) is normally present throughout entire recordings.

Reverse

Reverses the audio selection to provide an effect similar to playing an analogue tape backwards.

Silence

Replaces a selection with silence.

Stereo Flip

Allows you to manipulate the left and right channels in various ways. As you would expect, this function works only with stereo audio selections.

Time Stretch

Allows you to change the length and speed of the selected audio without affecting the pitch.

Plug-ins

All installed effect plug-ins are available separately on the Audio menu, and this allows you to apply effects processing to one or several selected events.

Spectrum Analyzer

Analyses the selected audio, computes the average 'spectrum' (level distribution over the frequency range) and displays this as a two-dimensional graph, with frequency on the X axis and level on the Y axis.

Statistics

Analyses the selected audio (events, clips or selection ranges) and displays a window with various information.

Hitpoints

A special feature that detects transient attacks in audio material and adds a type of marker, or hitpoint, at each attack. Once the hitpoints have been correctly set, you can slice up the file, which amongst other things enables you to change the tempo without affecting the pitch.

Detect Silence

Searches for silent sections in an event and either splits the event, removing the silent parts from the project, or creates regions corresponding to the non-silent sections.

Event As Region

Available when one or several audio events are selected, this function creates a region in the corresponding clip, with the start and end position of the region determined by the start and end position of the event within the clip.

Event From Regions

If you've selected an audio event whose clip contains regions within the boundaries of the event, this function will remove the original event and replace it with events positioned and sized according to the regions.

Create Regions

Allows you to create a region based on the current selection in the Sample Editor.

Events To Part

Allows you to create a part from selected audio events.

Close Gaps

Primarily intended to work with the Hitpoints feature and close the gaps created when playing back an audio file that has been sliced for tempo changes at a tempo lower than that of the original material.

Dissolve Part

Dissolves a selected audio part and makes any contained audio events appear as independent objects on the track.

Snap Point To Cursor

Sets the Snap point to the current cursor position.

Bounce Selection

Creates either a new clip or a new audio file from a selection.

Crossfade

Used to create a crossfade between two selected consecutive audio events. If the two events overlap, the crossfade will be applied to the overlapping area. If they don't overlap, but their respective audio clips do, the events are resized and a crossfade is applied in the overlapping range.

Remove Fades

Removes any fades or crossfades from a selected event.

Open Fade Editors

Opens the Fade dialog for a selected event. (Note that this will open two dialogs if the event has both fade-in and fade-out curves.)

Find Selected In Pool

Can be used to find the clips in the Pool for events selected in the Project window quickly. When this menu item is selected, the Pool opens with the corresponding clips highlighted.

Adjust Fades To Range

Allows you to adjust a fade area according to a range selection.

Offline Process History

Opens the Offline Process History dialog, where you can remove some or all processing previously applied to a clip.

Freeze Edits

Allows you to make permanent any processing or applied effects for a clip.

MIDI menu

Open Key Editor

Opens the Key Editor - a piano-roll-type graphic interface, with the notes shown as boxes in a grid - for a selected MIDI Part.

Open Score Editor

Opens the Score Editor, where MIDI data is interpreted as a musical score.

Open Drum Editor

Opens the Drum Editor, which is designed especially for editing drum and percussion tracks.

Open List Editor

Opens the List Editor and shows MIDI notes, controllers and other events as a list.

Over Quantize

Quantizing is a function that automatically moves recorded notes, positioning them on exact note values. This command quantizes the selected MIDI parts or notes according to the current setting in the Quantize pop-up menu.

Iterative Quantize

Instead of moving a note to the closest position on the quantize grid, Iterative Quantize moves it only part of the way. Specify how far the notes should be moved towards the grid with the Iterative Strength setting in the Quantize Setup dialog.

Quantize Setup

Use this to make various quantize settings.

Advanced Quantize

Quantize Lengths
This function is available only from within the MIDI editors and will quantize the length of the notes without changing their start positions. At its most basic level, this function will set the length of the notes to the Length Quantize value on the MIDI editor's toolbar.

Quantize Ends
Affects only the end positions of notes. Apart from that, it works just like regular quantizing, taking the setting in the Quantize pop-up menu as a reference.

Undo Quantize
Independent from the regular Undo History, this reverts the selected MIDI notes to their original, unquantized state at any time.

Freeze Quantize
Used when you want to make the quantized positions permanent. For example, you might want to quantize notes a second time, having the results based on the current quantized positions rather than the original positions. To make this possible, select the notes in question and use this function.

Transpose

This opens the Transpose dialog, where you can transpose selected notes.

Merge MIDI in Loop

Combines all MIDI events between the left and right locators on all unmuted tracks and generates a new MIDI part containing all of the events as you would hear them play back. The new part ends up on the selected track, between the locators. You're asked whether you want Cubase to include MIDI insert effects and/or send effects and whether or not your want it to overwrite (erase) the data on the destination track. A typical use for this is in freezing the settings you've made in the MIDI Track Inspector.

Dissolve Part

This item has two uses: to separate events according to MIDI channel when a MIDI part contains events on different channels (MIDI channel 'Any') and to separate MIDI events according to pitch. (Drum tracks typically have separate drum sounds for each pitch.)

O-Note Conversion

Available only if a drum map has been assigned for the MIDI track. Goes through the selected MIDI parts and sets the actual pitch of each note according to its O-note setting. Useful if you want to convert the track to a regular MIDI track with no drum map and still have the notes play back the correct drum sounds.

Functions menu

Legato

Extends each selected note so that it reaches the next note. Specify the desired gap or overlap with the Legato Overlap setting in the Preferences dialog box.

Fixed Lengths

Available only from within the MIDI editors, this resizes all selected notes to the length set within the Length Quantize pop-up menu on the MIDI editors' toolbars.

Delete Doubles

Removes double notes (notes of the same pitch at the exact same position), which can be produced when recording in Cycle mode, after quantizing, etc. This function always affects whole MIDI parts.

Delete Controllers

Removes all non-note events from the selected MIDI parts. This function always affects whole MIDI parts.

Delete Notes

Allows you to delete very short or weak notes. Particularly useful for automatically removing unwanted 'ghost notes' after recording.

Restrict Polyphony

Opens a dialog in which you can specify how many 'voices' should be used for the selected notes or parts. Restricting the polyphony this way is useful when you have an instrument with limited polyphony and want to make sure that all notes will be played. The effect is achieved by shortening notes as required so that they end before the next note starts.

Pedals To Note Length

Scans for sustain pedal on/off events, lengthens the affected notes to match the sustain pedal's 'off' position and then removes the sustain controller's on/off events.

Delete Overlaps (mono)

Allows you to make sure that no two notes of the same pitch overlap, ie that one starts before the other ends. (Overlapping notes of the same pitch can confuse some MIDI instruments.)

Delete Overlaps (poly)

Shortens notes when required so that no note begins before another ends. This happens regardless of pitch.

Velocity

Allows you to manipulate the velocity of notes in a variety of ways.

Fixed Velocity

Sets the velocity of all selected notes to the Insert Velocity value on the toolbar in the MIDI editors.

Reverse

Inverts the order of selected events, or of all events in selected parts, causing the MIDI music to play backwards. However, the effect is different from reversing an audio recording since, with MIDI, individual notes will still play as usual on the MIDI instrument; only the order of playback is changed. This function sets the velocity of all selected notes to the Insert Velocity value on the toolbar in the MIDI editors.

Logical Editor

Allows you to perform advanced search-and-replace operations on MIDI data.

Logical Presets

Contains various presets for use with the Logical Editor.

Drum Map Setup

The place where you load, create, modify and save drum maps. The list to the left shows the currently loaded drum maps. When you select a drum map in the list, its sounds and settings are displayed on the right-hand side.

Reset

Sends out Note Off messages and resets controllers on all MIDI channels. You can use this if you experience things like hanging notes or stuck controllers.

Pool menu

Import Medium

Used for importing files directly into the Pool. It's only available from the Pool menu when the Pool is open.

Import Audio CD

Opens a dialog that allows you to import audio from audio CDs.

Import Pool

Steinberg's Nuendo application can export the Pool as a separate file (file extension .npl), and such Pool files can be imported into Cubase SX by using the 'Import Pool' command on the Pool menu. When you import a Pool file, the file references in it are added to the current Pool. Audio and video files themselves are not saved in the Pool file; only a reference to them is stored. For there to be any point in importing a Pool file, you need access to all reference files, which preferably should have the same file paths as they had when the Pool was saved.

Find Missing Files

Opens the Resolve Missing Files dialog box, which can be used to find referenced files that may have been moved or renamed. Select 'Search' if you want the program to try to find the file for you, 'Locate' if you want to do it yourself or 'Folder' if you want to specify in which directory the program should search for the file.

Remove Missing Files

Removes all missing files from the Pool and removes their corresponding events from the Project window.

Reconstruct

If a missing file cannot be found - for instance, if you've accidentally deleted it from the hard disk - this will normally be indicated with a question mark next to the filename in the Status column in the Pool. However, if the missing file is an edit file created when you processed audio, stored in the 'Edits' folder within the project folder, it may be possible for the program to reconstruct it by recreating the editing carried out on the original audio file.

Convert Files

Opens the Convert Options dialog box, which operates on selected files. Use the pop-up menus to specify which attributes of an audio file you want to keep and which you want to convert.

Conform Files

Changes all selected files that have different attributes to conform to the standard specified for a project.

Create Folder

Creates a new audio subfolder and designates it as your 'Pool Record' folder.

Empty Trash

Self-explanatory.

Remove Unused Media

Finds all clips in the Pool that aren't used in a project and either moves them to the Pool Trash folder, where they can be permanently deleted, or removes them from the Pool.

Prepare Archive

When you want to archive a project, this checks that every clip referenced in the project is located in the same folder.

Set Pool Record Folder

Used to designate a new Pool Record folder. Just select the folder and choose this command to change the Pool Record folder to the selected folder.

Minimise File

Allows you to change the sizes of audio files according to the audio clips referenced in a project. Files produced using this option will contain only the portions of the audio file actually used in the project, which can significantly reduce the size of a project.

Update Origin

The original start position where a clip was recorded in the project is shown in the Pool's Origin Time column. As this value can be used as a basis for the Pool's Insert Into Project command and other functions, you can change it if the Origin Time value is redundant. This can be done by selecting the corresponding clip in the Pool, moving the Project cursor to the new desired position and selecting this menu item.

New Version

Allows you to create a new version of a selected clip. The new version appears in the same Pool folder, with the same name but with a version number after it to indicate that the new clip is a duplicate. However, copying a clip doesn't create a new file on disk, just a new version of the clip referring to the same original file.

Insert Into Project

Allows you to insert into a project clips selected in the Pool. Either the Origin Time value or the current cursor position can be used to determine where the clips are inserted (selected on the submenu for this menu item).

Select In Project

Tells you which events in a project refer to a particular clip in the Pool. Select the clip in the Pool and then select the command. The corresponding event(s) will be selected in the Project window.

Find In Pool

Performs a search of the Pool to locate particular clips or regions. You can specify various criteria to match in the dialog that pops up.

Transport menu

Transport Panel

Opens the Transport panel.

Locators To Selection

Sets the locators to encompass the currently selected range.

Locate Selection

Moves the Project cursor to the start of the currently selected range.

Locate Next Marker

Moves the Project cursor to the next marker position.

Locate Previous Marker

Moves the Project cursor to the previous marker position.

Locate Next Event

Moves the Project cursor to the start or end of the next event on the selected track.

Locate Previous Event

Moves the Project cursor to the start or end of the previous event on the selected track.

Play From Selection Start

Moves the Project cursor to the start of the current selection and activates playback.

Play From Selection End

Moves the Project cursor to the end of the current selection and activates playback.

Play Until Selection Start

Activates playback two seconds before the start of the currently selected range and stops at the selection start.

Play Until Selection End

Activates playback two seconds before the end of the selected range and stops at the selection end.

Play Until Next Marker

Activates playback from the Project cursor's position until the next marker.

Play Selection Range

Plays back the current selection range.

Loop Selection

Loops the playback of the current selection range.

Use Pre/Post-Roll

If this is ticked, Pre/Post-Roll is activated.

Start Record At Left Locator

If ticked, the Project cursor will jump to the left locator's position and begin recording when you hit the Record button. If unticked, recording will start directly from the Project cursor's current position.

Metronome Setup

Opens the Metronome Setup dialog, where you can input various metronome settings.

Metronome On

Activates the metronome.

Sync Setup

Opens a dialog box where settings relating to synchronisation can be made.

Sync Online

Activates synchronisation.

Devices menu

MIDI Device Manager

Allows you to install MIDI devices so that you can either select pre-configured MIDI devices from a list or define a device from scratch.

Mixer

Opens the Mixer, where all audio, MIDI and group tracks in a project are displayed with a corresponding channel strip, as are any activated VST instrument and ReWire channels. The Master bus fader can also be shown in the Mixer.

Plug-in Information

Lists all installed VST, DirectX and MIDI plug-ins and shows various information about them.

TrueTape

A unique Steinberg technology that emulates the behaviour of a professional analogue tape recorder. If activated when during audio recording, TrueTape can be viewed as a separate recording mode.

VST Inputs

Opens the VST Inputs window, which allows you to activate audio inputs connected to your audio hardware.

VST Instruments

Opens the VST Instruments window, where you can select up to 32 VST instruments. With MIDI tracks, when a VST instrument has been selected for a slot in the window, the corresponding plug-in is selectable as a destination on the MIDI Output pop-up menu.

VST Master Effects

Up to eight master effects can be added to the signal on the Master bus. The last two effect slots are post Master gain, which is useful for dithering plug-ins.

VST Master Setup

Opens the VST Master Setup dialog, which is used for selecting various surround configurations.

VST Outputs

Shows the output buses connected to the physical outputs on your audio hardware.

VST Performance

Indicates the computer's current CPU load and disk transfer rate.

VST Send Effects

Used for selecting up to eight global send effects.

Video

Opens the default video player in the Device Setup dialog.

Show Panel

Opens a panel on which you can select directly any of the devices currently on the Device menu.

Device Setup

Allows you to add or remove remote-control devices and to make various basic settings for audio and MIDI, such as selecting ASIO drivers and MIDI ports.

microphone magic

When it comes to serious recording, you can never over-emphasise the importance of microphones. Microphones convert the sounds that you hear into electrical signals that can be recorded, and, as mentioned earlier in the book, choosing the right mic for the musical genre at hand is critically important to getting the sound you want on your final tracks. No amount of EQ, compression or reverb can change the subtle signature that any particular microphone leaves on an audio track.

So how do you choose that perfect mic without buying and auditioning everything on the market? For a start, you could talk to other musicians and producers to find out what has worked for them in the past and what sort of mics they'd recommend, and reviews in magazines like *Sound On Sound* are always worth a look. Before you start shopping around for anything, however, make sure that you're familiar with the basic microphone 'families'. These include mics used for recording vocals and instrumentation.

To begin with, microphone pick-up patterns include *omnidirectional*, *cardioid*, *figure of eight* and *stereo*, while the types of pick-up themselves include *dynamic*, *condenser* and *ribbon*.

pick-up patterns

Omnidirectional
An omnidirectional mic picks up sound equally from all directions. Omni mics tend to have a very good bass response, without the artificial low-frequency boost provided by the proximity effect picked up by a typical cardioid mic. (The proximity effect determines that, the closer a sound source is to a cardioid mic, the more the mic will accentuate that sound source's bass-frequency output.) This can add richness and fullness to a singer's voice or to a saxophone's sound, but it can also muddy the sound of a guitar amp or acoustic bass.

Really good omnidirectional condenser mics are great at capturing a sense of open space and air, which makes them the first choice for critical reproduction of acoustic instruments – such as symphonic orchestras, vocal choirs, pianos or string quartets – in good-sounding acoustic spaces like concert halls. You can also use omnidirectional microphones to close mic an instrument or vocalist without worrying about the artificial bass boost caused by the proximity effect picked up by a directional mic.

Some of the highest-fidelity mics available are of the omnidirectional condenser variety, including models from Schoeps, DPA (B&K) and Earthworks.

Cardioid

A cardioid mic is more sensitive to sounds directly in front of it than it is to sounds 90 degrees off to either side and is even less sensitive to sounds directly behind it. In fact, cardioid mics practically cancel out any sounds that emanate from directly behind the mic. This makes them very useful for PA and live recording use and the most popular choice for use in the imperfect recording environments of most home digital studios. To use a cardioid mic, simply aim the mic at the instrument that you want to record and the rest of the stage sound will be at least somewhat quieter than the desired instrument's sound. Most of today's most popular microphones have a cardioid pick-up pattern.

There are also a couple of variations on the cardioid pick-up pattern. Supercardioid and hypercardioid mics are less sensitive to 90° off-axis sources than plain cardioids, which means that they'll do a better job of rejecting sounds from off to the sides. However, hypercardioids pick up some sound from directly behind the front of the mic, which makes them a little bit like figure-of-eight mics (see below), and cardioid mics in general also pick up the proximity effect.

When miking from a distance, cardioid mics have a tendency to sound somewhat thin in the bass when compared to omnidirectional mics. For this reason, cardioid mics are usually used for close miking, with the mic placed less than two feet away from the sound source, while omnidirectional or figure-of-eight mics are usually used when miking from farther away.

Figure Of Eight

Figure-of-eight mics have the 'open' sound and good bass response of omnidirectional mics with the added advantage of rejecting sounds from either side of the mic. Since figure-of-eight mics pick up sound equally well from directly behind and directly in front of the mic, you should take care that you don't capture undesirable reflections from low ceilings or nearby walls. A good place to use a figure-of-eight-pattern mic is when you need to cancel reflections from side walls in a narrowish room but you still want to capture a good sense of room ambience.

pick-up types

Dynamic

Dynamic mics use a moving coil to sense the changes in air pressure that make sound waves. The wire coil is suspended over a permanent magnet, and when moving air hits the coil the air causes it to move over the magnet, prompting a process called *electromagnetic induction* to take place. This causes an AC voltage to be formed that is electrically analogous to the original sound. The electrical signal that appears at the mic's output is a fairly faithful reproduction of the original vibrations in air, only in fluctuating AC voltages instead of air-pressure changes.

Small-Diaphragm Dynamic

These are by far the most commonly used mics for PA and stage sound use. Dynamic microphones are typically very rugged and don't require a voltage source to work properly. Cardioid-pattern small-diaphragm dynamic mics are most often used as hand-held vocal mics (such as the ubiquitous Shure SM-58) or as instrument mics for stage use (like the equally ubiquitous Shure SM-57). There are many other similar dynamic mics available from companies like Audix, Electro-Voice, Sennheiser and many others.

Large-Diaphragm Dynamic

While similar to their small-diaphragm siblings, large-diaphragm dynamic mics are typically used for very loud, bass-heavy instruments such as tom-toms, kick drums and bass-amp speakers. The larger diaphragm allows these mics to withstand higher SPLs (Sound Pressure Levels) with ease, which allows low-distortion sound reproduction. However, the larger diaphragm will also weigh more and has a higher moving mass, which can limit the high-frequency response and transient response of the mic. Some popular large-diaphragm dynamic mics include the following:

- Electro-Voice RE-20 - A favourite of radio announcers and a good mic for kick drums;

- Shure SM-7 - Similar to the Electro-Voice RE-20;

- Sennheiser MD-421 - Commonly used on tom-toms and hand percussion;

- Shure SM7 - A large-diaphragm dynamic mic used for broadcasts and voice-overs as well as for miking kick drums and brass and bass instruments.

Condenser

A condenser mic captures sound by using a conductive diaphragm with a capacitative charged plate behind it. The charge is supplied by a DC voltage source such as a battery or the 48V phantom power supply present in most mixers and mic pre-amps. Air-pressure changes meeting the conductive diaphragm cause it to move, which in turn causes an analogous AC voltage to be formed in the charged plate. These tiny AC voltages are sent to a small pre-amp built into the microphone, which brings the signal up to the level at which it can drive a typical microphone pre-amp. The signal leaves the microphone via the cable and is sent to the microphone pre-amplifier stage of the mixer. Because their diaphragms can be made very thin and light, condenser mics tend to be more accurate and 'faster' than dynamic mics, especially in the mid-range and treble frequencies. However, they also tend to be more physically delicate than dynamic mics, so they're more commonly used for studio recording than for live sound and PA situations. There are a few condenser mics specially designed to withstand the rough and tumble of stage use, such as the Shure SM-87.

Small-Diaphragm Condenser

Small-diaphragm condenser mics have the best high-frequency response and quickest transient response of all of the commonly available types of microphone. For this reason, small-diaphragm condenser mics are most often used as drum kit overhead mics to faithfully capture cymbals and stick attacks, for acoustic stringed instruments such as guitars and violins and for percussion instruments such as vibraphones, shakers and marimbas. Another common use for small-diaphragm condenser mics is as stereo pairs to pick up ambient acoustic events in good-sounding spaces. However, the one downside to small-diaphragm condensers is that they tend to be noisier than other types of microphone.

Popular small-diaphragm condenser mics include the following:

• Shure SM-81 – A mic with a very flat frequency response, commonly used on acoustic guitars and as a drum kit overhead mic;

• Audio Technica AT-3528 – A cardioid model that is a sort of a poor man's KM-84;

• AKG C 1000 S – A good all-round budget favourite;

• Neumann KM184 – A truly professional recording mic;

• Oktava MC-012 – From Russia, this is another mic designed to be similar to the KM-84 but cheaper;

• Earthworks QTC-1 – Another great professional mic with an extremely accurate response.

Large-Diaphragm Condenser

Since condenser mics are intrinsically more sensitive to higher frequencies, it's possible to combine the warmth and fullness of a large diaphragm with the high-frequency detail typical of a small-diaphragm condenser mic in a single microphone. These large-diaphragm condenser mics are the mainstay of recording studios everywhere, especially for recording vocals, pianos, horns and other acoustic instruments. Some older vacuum-tube-based large-diaphragm condenser mics, such as the Neumann U47 and AKG C12, are collector's items and prized for their sonic warmth and smoothly accurate reproduction of aural details. The 1960s vintage Neumann U87 is an FET-amplified large-diaphragm mic that is more of a modern classic...and well beyond the budgets of most home studios.

Some of the more popular large-diaphragm condenser microphones include the following:

• AKG CS 414 ULS – an industry standard for overhead drum miking and general use, providing a choice of cardioid, hypercardioid, omni and figure-of-eight pick-up patterns

• AKG C 3000 B – A budget mic based on the design of the venerable CS 414 (cardioid only)

• Neumann U87 – The standard by which all others are judged, providing a choice of cardioid, hypercardioid, omnidirectional and figure-of-eight pick-up patterns

• Neumann TLM 103 – A new, lower-priced version of the famous U87 (cardioid only)

• Audio Technica AT-4033A – A fabulous microphone for the price (cardioid only, and great on saxophones)

Ribbon

By suspending a small, wafer-thin aluminium ribbon between two mounting points inside a strong magnetic field, you get a microphone that is extraordinarily sensitive to vibrations in the air. Ribbon mics can really capture the thump of a plucked acoustic bass or the subtle dynamics of jazz drums. Unfortunately, ribbon mics tend to be extraordinarily fragile; blow on the ribbon the wrong way and you can stretch it out beyond repair. Nevertheless, ribbon mics remain a favourite amongst well-heeled recordists everywhere.

Common ribbon mics include the following:

- RCA BX-44 and BX-77 – The original classics

- Coles 4038 – Sets the standard of modern ribbon mics

- Beyerdynamic M-260 – a budget ribbon mic (hypercardioid only)

- Royer Labs R-121 – A new ribbon mic design that's getting a lot of attention

Stereo

If you combine two cardioid condenser elements in one chassis, you get a single-point stereo mic. This is usually an X-Y type, where the two cardioid elements are pointed away from each other at a 90-degree angle. Some stereo mics are of the mid-side type, using a combination of a forward-facing cardioid element with sideways-oriented figure-of-eight element, which allows you to remotely control adjustments of the stereo-image width.

Popular stereo mics include the following:

- Audio Technica AT-825

- Shure VP-88

- Crown SASS

vocal versus instrument mics

Vocal Mics

Recording the human singing or speaking voice presents some unique challenges. Most people prefer a heightened sense of presence on the human voice and will often also prefer a mild bass boost for added warmth. As a result, most microphones meant for recording or amplifying vocals have a tailored response characteristic. Dynamic vocal mics are designed to be very sturdy and to produce as little handling noise as possible. They are also designed with a very tight cardioid or hypercardioid pick-up pattern so that there is minimal bleed from other instruments on the stage. As mentioned earlier, the standard mic of this type is the Shure SM58, which can withstand very rough treatment and has very good feedback rejection, making it perfect for daily use on stages where amplified rock, pop, R&B or jazz bands play. The SM58 has a specially tailored response that reduces bass pick-up from far away, thus minimising booming from the stage sound, but it will boost the bass when the singer comes in close, creating a big, warm sound. The SM58 has a substantial peak in its response from about 2kHz up to about 12kHz, which adds a pleasant sheen and an overall brightness to the sound. This helps vocals cut through a dense mix and increases clarity and intelligibility.

You can usually tell if a microphone is designed for live sound vocal use by checking to see if it's equipped with a pop filter to protect the pick-up from blasts of air on plosive sounds. The Shure SM58 has a spherical metal screen pop filter that is lined with foam rubber on the inside.

When recording vocals, most studios use large-diaphragm condenser microphones like the Neumann U87 or AKG C12. Like stage mics, these also have a presence peak and proximity effect tailored to enhance the sound of the vocalist. However, because these large-diaphragm condenser microphones are to be used in the more controlled environment of a recording studio, they can have wider cardioid pick-up patterns, allowing for a more open sound.

When choosing a mic to record a particular musical genre, you'll need to pick your microphone like a musician picks his instrument. For example, a darker mic will help to tame a high, shrill voice, while a clearer, brighter-sounding mic will help the vocal cut through a dense mix. Unfortunately, there is no single best microphone for all situations, only a palette of good microphones from which you have to choose the right tool for the job at hand. The standard large-diaphragm vocal mic is the Neumann U87, although some prefer the vacuum-tube-based Neumann U47. These microphones have a distinctive upper-mid range to treble/presence boost and a warm, rich bass boost via their tendency to pick up the proximity effect. Similar mics to the U47 and U87 are the AKG C12 and CS 414 ULS, both of which have the crisper sound characteristic of AKG microphones in general, which some producers love and others hate. There is an increasing number of less expensive versions of these microphones on the market today, including mics like the following:

- RØDE NT1000

- Audio Technica AT-4033a, AT-4047

- AKG C2000S, C3000B

- Marshall Electronics MXL-2001-P

- Joe Meek Meekrophone

- Oktava MC-319

When you use a condenser mic to record a vocalist, it's usually a good idea to hang a pop screen between the vocalist and the microphone to keep loud 'p', 'b' and 'k' sounds from overloading the mic's pick-up and spoiling a take. You can buy these or make them out of an old pair of tights and a tea strainer.

Instrument Mics

When it comes to recording instruments, different priorities arise, depending on your musical genre and style. When recording acoustic instruments, the microphone should be faithful to the original sound. However, instruments used in rock and pop music can be very loud and require a mic that can withstand extremely high sound pressure levels without distorting. It's extremely difficult to make a mic that's both sensitive enough to pick up the subtle nuances of a fine acoustic instrument while also being able to capture the brute force of a rock kick drum or guitar amp without overloading. Once again, there's no single best mic for all situations, and you'll have to base your choice on what you have to record and what mics are available.

Dynamic mics are best for loud sounds such as rock drum kits, guitar amplifiers and close-miked brass instruments. There are a select few dynamic microphones around that are both rugged and have a smooth sound that's suitable for recording high-decibel musical instruments, but be aware that typically these are more expensive than dynamic vocal microphones and don't work as well as condenser types on instruments with complex high-frequency information. The Sennheisser 421 and 422 and the Beyerdynamic M88 are among the most widely used of this type of dynamic instrument microphone, while the Electro-Voice RE-20 is also popular. The Shure SM57 is frequently used on snare drums, hand percussion (congas, bongos, timbales, etc) and guitar amplifiers but not usually for bass-heavy instruments like kick drums or electric bass guitars. You'll usually see dynamic microphones used for live stage performances, while condenser mics are more often used in the recording studio.

When choosing a condenser mic, again the type must be chosen to match the sonic characteristics of the source that you want to record. Orchestral instruments, acoustic stringed instruments and classical music ensembles will usually be recorded with sensitive condenser microphones that have relatively flat frequency responses. It's generally acknowledged that small-diaphragm condenser mics such as those from DPA, Schoeps and Earthworks provide the most accurate response, while some prefer the pleasant-sounding colouration of the large-diaphragm Neumann M50 or similar.

close-miking individual acoustic instruments

When recording an individual brass, wind or reed instrument for a pop or jazz recording, a large-diaphragm condenser microphone such as a Neumann U87 or AKG CS 414 ULS will often be used. If recording a featured solo, the instrumentalist is treated similarly to a vocalist – ie the microphone may be chosen as much for its desirable colourations as for its clarity, warmth, headroom or lack of distortion. Acoustic piano is treated in several different ways, depending on the style of music and the sound quality desired. A solo classical piano is usually miked from a considerable distance away, with careful attention paid to the quality of the room's acoustics and the degree to which the microphones pick up the ambient sound of the room compared to the more direct sound of the instrument. Often, an X-Y stereo pair of condenser mics will be used. For rock, pop or jazz piano in a group, the instrument will often be miked much closer, often with the lid closed and the piano isolated from the room sound with sound-absorbing blankets. For a robust, rich sound, choose a large-diaphragm condenser mic; for a brighter, clear sound, choose a small-diaphragm model.

Drum Kits

For rock and pop, the individual pieces of the drum kit are usually miked individually. This allows greater freedom at the mixdown stage to alter the sound to taste. As a general guideline, try the following set-up:

- **Snare Drum** – The most common technique is to place a Shure SM57 so that it picks up the sound from the batter (top) head. Sometimes a second microphone is placed underneath the drum to pick up the sound of the snare wires. The output from this microphone may need to be reversed in polarity so that it doesn't introduce phase cancellations with the signal from the top snare mic;

- **Kick Drum** – Depending on the sound of the kick drum itself, a large-diaphragm dynamic mic such as an Electro-Voice RE-20 may be placed close to the centre of the front drumhead or inside the drum, if the front head has a hole in it or has been removed. Experimentation with placement will be necessary to achieve the desired sound;

- **Cymbals** – In most cases, a stereo pair of condenser microphones will be placed at least two feet above the kit to capture the sound of the cymbals and the overall sound of the drum kit. Where it's desired to capture the sound of the tom-toms with the overhead mic pair, it's usually best to use large-diaphragm condenser microphones. (The AKG CS 414 works well here.) If the tom-toms are close-miked, it's usually best to use small-diaphragm condenser mics so that the low mids don't build up to an unusable degree. Suitable small-diaphragm condenser mics include the AKG C1000S, the Audio Technica AT-4041, the Neumann KM-184 and the Oktava MC012;

- **Tom-Toms** – If desired, the individual tom-toms can be close-miked with a large-diaphragm dynamic microphone such as the Sennheisser 421, while small clip-on condenser mics such as the Shure Beta 98 are also used. Take care to place the microphones so that they won't cause phase cancellations or introduce excessive bleed between tracks.

In the 1950s and 1960s, drum kits were often miked with only two microphones, one a couple of feet or so in front of the kit and the other a couple of feet overhead and pointed at the snare drum. Ribbon mics like the RCA BX-77 or Coles 4038 were often used, as well as the newer large-diaphragm condenser mics such as the Neumann U67. While you won't get a stereo spread with this set-up, it is possible to get a very accurate picture of the acoustic sound of the drum kit. This can be a very effective technique for making live recordings of jazz groups.

fixes

I f you were an early adapter, you might not be currently running the most recent version of Cubase SX, and by the time you buy this book there will probably be several more version updates as well. However, at the time of writing, Cubase SX 1.02 has come onstream to replace version 1.01 and can be downloaded from the Internet. You can use Cubase SX's Update tool for automatic downloading or you can browse to the updater manually by visiting http://service.steinberg.net/webdoc.nsf/show/updates_pc_e

To give you some idea of what you'll be getting, here's a quick run-down of new and fixed features.

new

- Channel sets can be organised in 'Mixer View Presets'. Check out the pop-up on the lower edge of mixer control strip – here you can add and remove your choice of visible channels.

- Two mixers are now available for use with different mixer views. Simply select from the two menu options that are now available on the Devices menu. Unused or unwanted MIDI ports can be marked as not shown in the Device Setup panel; they will then not be shown in any MIDI Port input/output pop-up.

- SMPTE sub-frames can be added to the Timecode displays. There is a switch for this on the 'Transport' page in the Preferences dialog.

- Now the Zoom presets on the Project window's horizontal scaler has a new 'Organise' option. This allows the Zooms to be rename and deleted.

- The cycle sets (part of the marker track) appear on this list. Once these are clicked, the screen is automatically zoomed and positioned to this cycle range.

- If cycle markers – as they appear on a marker track – are double-clicked with [Alt] held down, the project window is zoomed and positioned to just this range.

- Houston now displays MIDI and audio channels, just as can be seen on the screen. The new Mixer View Presets can be switched via Houston (sets plus numeric pad). Houston can 'flip faders', where the functionality of the rotary encoders and faders can be swapped, by pressing [Shift] + motors. This is great for 'touch fader' automation of other parameters.

- [Shift] + Edit – closes a window

- [Shift] + Save – creates a new (incremental) back-up copy.

- [Shift] + Undo – opens the Edit History, while there's also a new MIDI-only bank added to the pop-up menu.

fixes
Project window

- Save of inactive projects now works correctly

- Solo/Mute logic is now working as expected (multiple MIDI tracks routed to the same MIDI device previously caused erratic behaviour during unmuting/unsoloing)

- No more crashing when recording audio and MIDI simultaneously

- Editing event-start points by changing values in the Info line now works correctly

- System crash that often occurred when an the Audio editor was closed during playback has been fixed

- Speaker tool in Part editor now works when editor's Solo function is activated

- Song position pointer doesn't disappear in the Audio Part editor any more

- Range tool now works properly after Scissors have been selected

- Parts are now deselected when a new track is created

Mixer

- Hidden status of channels can now be turned off again

- The attribute 'hidden' has been renamed 'hideable' to better match its purpose

remote controls

- Tascam US428 knobs can now be configured

- Jog wheel now works during playback

ReWire/Reason

- No more MIDI-note 'burst' in certain situations

VST System Link, transport, sync

- MIDI transmission to second VST System Link computer now works correctly

- Incoming full-frame message now filtered automatically when sending MMC

- Cycle On/Off during playback now works correctly

audio editors

- The Speaker tool in the Audio Part editor is optimised. It now plays the selected events on all lanes and locks magnetically to a part or plays the whole part when the hold [Ctrl] key is held down

MIDI editors

- Controller lane in editors – no more value changes from already existing data after a new event is created with the Pencil tool

Drum Editor

- Self-created quantize pattern now works on Drumstick stroke

- Snap Off now working on drumstick

- No more problems with wrongly routed notes when drum maps are used.

Score Editor

- Vertical scroll in Edit mode now works in all situations

- Opening layouts that contain tracks in folders now works

- Flipping tuplets now saved

- System crash that occurred when closing the note-head pop-up with window gadget now fixed.

- Various spelling errors corrected

- Tool Tips in the Score status bar have been added

Steinberg is constantly making improvements and fixing minor glitches in Cubase SX, so it's definitely worth keeping an eye on their website for version updates. Cubase SX makes updating from downloads reasonably easy, so there's no reason to be running an out-of-date system.

glossary

absorption

Short for the term acoustical absorption, the quality of a surface or substance that takes in a sound wave rather than reflecting it.

acoustic amplifier

The portion of an instrument that makes the vibrating source move more air or move air more efficiently, making the sound of the instrument louder. Examples of acoustic amplifiers include the body of an acoustic guitar, the soundboard of a piano, the bell of a horn and the shell of a drum.

acoustic echo chamber

A room designed with very hard, non-parallel surfaces and equipped with a speaker and microphone. Dry signals from the console are fed to the speaker and the microphone will have a reverberation of these signals that can be mixed in with the dry signals at the console.

A/D

Abbreviation of either *analogue-to-digital conversion* (ie the conversion of a quantity that has continuous changes into numbers that approximate those changes) or *analogue-to-digital converter*.

ADAT

A trademark of Alesis for its modular digital multitrack recording system, released in early 1993.

ADSR

Abbreviation for *attack, decay, sustain* and *release*, the various elements of volume changes in the sounding of a keyboard instruments, and also the four segments of a common type of synthesiser envelope. The controls for these four parameters determine the duration (or, in the case of sustain, the height) of the segments of the envelope.

AES/EBU

A standard professional interface for sending and receiving digital audio adopted by the Audio Engineering Society and the European Broadcast Union.

AIFF

Abbreviation of *audio interchange file format*, a common format for Macintosh audio files. It can be mono or stereo, and at a sampling rate of up to 48kHz. AIFF files are compatible with QuickTime.

algorithm

A set of procedures designed to accomplish something. In the case of computer software, the procedures may appear to the user as a configuration of software components – for example, an arrangement of operators in a Yamaha DX-series synthesiser – or as an element (such as a reverb algorithm) that performs specific operations on a signal.

aliasing

Undesired frequencies that are produced when harmonic components within the audio signal being sampled by a digital recording device or generated within a digital sound source lie above the Nyquist frequency. Aliasing differs from some other types of noise in that its pitch changes radically when the pitch of the intended sound changes. On playback, the system will provide a signal at an incorrect frequency, called an alias frequency. Aliasing is a kind of distortion.

All Notes Off

A MIDI command, recognised by some (but not all) synthesisers and sound modules, that causes any notes that are currently sounding to be shut off. The panic button on a synth or sequencer usually transmits All Notes Off messages on all 16 MIDI channels.

ambience

The portion of a sound that comes from the surrounding environment, rather than directly from the sound source.

ambient miking

Placing a microphone in the reverberant field in order to take a separate recording of the ambience or to allow the recording engineer to change the mix of direct to reverberant sound in the recording.

amplitude

The height of a waveform above or below the zero line, or the amount of a signal. Amplitude is measured by determining the amount of fluctuation in air pressure of a sound, the voltage of an electrical signal or, in a digital application, numerical data. When the signal is in the audible range, amplitude is perceived as loudness.

analogue

Representative, continuous changes that relate to another quantity that has a continuous change. Capable of exhibiting continuous fluctuations. In an analogue audio system, fluctuations in voltage correspond in a one-to-one fashion with (that is, are analogous to) the fluctuations in air pressure at the audio input or output. In an analogue synthesiser, parameters such as oscillator pitch and LFO speed are typically controlled by analogue control voltages, rather than by digital data, and the audio signal is also an analogue voltage.

analogue recording

A recording of the continuous changes of an audio waveform.

analogue-to-digital converter

A device which converts a quantity that has continuous changes (usually of voltage) into numbers that approximate those changes. Alternatively, a device that changes the continuous fluctuations in voltage from an analogue device (such as a microphone) into digital information that can be stored or processed in a sampler, digital signal processor or digital recording device.

attack

The first part of the sound of a note. In a synthesiser ADSR envelope, the attack segment is the segment during which the envelope rises from its initial value (usually zero) to the attack level (often the maximum level for the envelope) at a rate determined by the attack-time parameter.

attenuator

A potentiometer (pot) that is used to lower the amplitude of a signal passing through it. The amplitude can usually be set to any value between full (no attenuation) and zero (infinite attenuation). Pots can be either rotary or linear (sliders), and can be either hardware or virtual sliders on a computer screen.

automatic gain (volume) control

A compressor with a very long release time. Used to keep the volume of audio material constant.

automation

In consoles, automation is a feature that allows the engineer to program control changes (such as fader level) so that, on playback of the multitrack recording, these changes happen automatically.

aux send

Abbreviation of *auxiliary send*, which adjusts the level of a signal sent from the console input channel to the auxiliary equipment through the aux bus.

auxiliary equipment

Effects devices separate from but working with a recording console.

axis

A line around which a device operates. In a microphone, for example, this would be an imaginary line coming out of the front of the mic in the direction of the diaphragm's motion.

baffles

Sound-absorbing panels used to prevent sound waves from entering or leaving a certain space.

balance

1. The relative level of two or more instruments in a mix, or the relative level of audio signals in the channels of a stereo recording. 2. To even out the relative levels of audio signals in the channels of a stereo recording.

balance control

A control on a stereo amplifier that, when moved clockwise, makes the right channel louder and the left channel softer and will do the reverse when moved anticlockwise.

balanced

1. Having a pleasing amount of low frequencies when compared to mid-range frequencies and high frequencies. 2. Having a pleasing mixture of the various instrument levels in an audio recording. 3. Having a fairly equal level in each of the stereo channels. 4. A method of interconnecting electronic gear using three-conductor cables.

bandwidth

1. The range of frequencies over which a tape recorder, amplifier or other audio device is useful. 2. The range of frequencies affected by an equalisation setting - ie the available 'opening' through which information can pass. In audio, the bandwidth of a device is the portion of the frequency spectrum that it can handle without significant degradation taking place. In digital communications, the bandwidth is the amount of data that can be transmitted over a given period of time.

bank

1. A collection of sound patches (data concerned with the sequence and operating parameters of the synthesiser generators and modifiers) in computer memory. 2. A number of sound modules grouped together as a unit.

baud rate

Informally, the number of bits of computer information transmitted each second. MIDI transmissions have a baud rate of 31,250 (31.25 kilobaud), while modems typically have a much lower rate of 2,400, 9,600 or 14,400 baud.

bar

The same as the American term *measure*, ie the grouping of a number of beats in a music (most often four).

barrier miking

A method of placing the head of a microphone as close as possible to a reflective surface, thus preventing phase cancellation.

bass

1. The lower range of audio frequencies, up to approximately 250Hz. 2. Abbreviation of bass guitar.

bass roll-off

An electrical network built into some microphones to reduce the amount of output at bass frequencies when close-miking.

beat

1. A steady, even pulse in music. 2. The action of two sounds or audio signals mixing together and causing regular rises and falls in volume.

bi-directional pattern

A microphone pick-up pattern that has maximum pick-up directly in front and directly to the rear of the diaphragm and least pick-up at the sides.

bit

The smallest unit of digital information, representing a single zero or one. Digital audio is encoded in words that are usually eight, twelve or 16 bits long (ie the bit resolution). Each additional bit represents a theoretical improvement of about 6dB in the signal-to-noise ratio.

blending

1. A condition where two signals mix together to form one sound or give the sound of one sound source or one performance. 2. Mixing the left and right signal together slightly, which makes the instruments sound closer to the centre of the performance stage. 3. A method of panning during mixing where instruments are not panned extremely left or right.

board

1. Another, less formal, term for console or desk. 2. A set of controls and their housing which control all signals necessary for recording and mixing. 3. A slang shortening of the term *keyboard instrument*.

boom

1. A hand-held, telescoping pole used to suspend a microphone above a sound source when recording dialogue in film production. 2. A telescoping support arm attached to a microphone stand which holds the microphone. 3. Loosely, a boom stand.

BPM

Abbreviation of *beats per minute*.

brick-wall filter

A low-pass filter at the input of an analogue-to-digital converter. Used to prevent frequencies above the Nyquist frequency from being encoded by the converter.

buffer

Memory used for the recording or editing of data before it is stored in a more permanent form.

bulk dump

Short for *system-exclusive bulk dump*, a method of transmitting data, such as the internal parameters of a MIDI device to another MIDI device.

byte

A grouping of eight information bits.

capsule

1. The variable capacitor section of a condenser microphone. 2. In other types of microphone, the part of the microphone that includes the diaphragm and the active element.

card

1. A plug-in memory device. RAM cards, which require an internal battery, can be used for storing user data, while ROM cards, which have no battery, can only be used for reading the data recorded on them by the manufacturer. 2. A circuit board that plugs into a slot on a computer.

cardioid pattern

A microphone pick-up pattern which picks up most sound from the front, less from the sides and the least from the back of the diaphragm.

cascade

To set and interconnect two mixers so that the stereo mixing bus(es) of a mixer feed(s) the stereo bus(es) of a second mixer.

chamber

1. An echo chamber, ie a room designed with very hard, non-parallel surfaces equipped with a speaker and microphone so that, when dry signals from the console are fed to the speaker, the microphone picks up a reverberation of these signals, which can then be combined with the dry signals at the console. 2. A program in a delay/reverb effects device that simulates the sound of an echo chamber.

channel

1. In multitrack tape machines, the same as *track* (ie one audio recording made on a portion of the width of a multitrack tape). 2. A single path that an audio signal travels or can travel through a device from an input to an output.

chord

Two or more musical pitches sung or played together.

chorus

1. The part of a song that is repeated and has the same music and lyrics each time. The chorus usually gives the point of the song. 2. A musical singing group that has many singers. 3. A delay effect that simulates a vocal chorus by adding several delays with a mild amount of feedback and a medium amount of depth. 4. A similar effect created in some synthesisers by detuning (reducing the pitch slightly) and mixing it with a signal that has regular tuning and a slight delay.

chorusing

A type of signal processing. In chorusing, a time-delayed or detuned copy of a signal is mixed with the original signal. The mixing process changes the relative strengths and phase relationships of the overtones to create a fatter, more animated sound. The simplest way to achieve chorusing is by detuning one synthesiser oscillator from another to produce a slow beating between them.

clangorous

Containing partials that aren't part of the natural harmonic series. Clangorous tones often sound like bells.

clip

To deform a waveform during overload.

clock signal

The signal put out by a circuit that generates the steady, even pulses or codes used for synchronisation.

close miking

A technique involving placing a microphone close to (ideally within a foot of) a sound source being recorded in order to pick up primarily the direct sound and to avoid picking up leakage or ambience.

co-ax

Twin-conductor cable consisting of one conductor surrounded by a shield.

coincident microphones (coincident pair)

An arrangement by which the heads of two microphones are placed as close as possible to each other so that the path length from any sound source to either microphone is, for all practical purposes, the same.

compander

1. A two-section device used in noise-reduction systems. The first section compresses the

audio signal before it is recorded and the second section expands the signal after it's been recorded. 2. In Yamaha digital consoles, a signal processor that applies both compression and expansion to the same signal. Digital companding allows a device to achieve a greater apparent dynamic range with fewer bits per sample word (see *digital word*).

compressor

A signal-processing device that allows less fluctuation in the level of the signal above a certain adjustable or fixed level.

condenser

An old term meaning the same thing as *capacitor*, ie an electronic device that is composed of two plates separated by an insulator and can store charge. The term is still in common use when used to refer to a microphone's active element.

condenser microphone

A microphone that converts changes in sound pressure into changes in capacitance. The capacitance changes are then converted into variations in electrical voltage (ie an audio signal).

console

A set of controls and their housing that control all of the signals necessary for recording and mixing.

contact microphone

A device that senses vibrations and puts out an audio signal that is proportional to the vibrations.

controller

1. Any device - for example, a keyboard, wind synth controller or pitch-bend lever - capable of producing a change in some aspect of a sound by altering the action of some other device. 2. Any of the defined MIDI data types used for controlling the ongoing quality of a sustaining tone. (Strictly speaking, MIDI continuous controllers are numbered from 0 to 127.) In many synthesisers, the controller-data category is more loosely defined in order to include pitch-bend and aftertouch data. 3. Any device generating a control voltage or signal fed to another device's control input.

CPU (central processing unit)

1. The main 'brain' chip of a computer, which performs the calculations and execution of instructions. 2. The main housing of a computer containing the 'brain' chip, as opposed to other pieces of the computer system, such as keyboards, monitors, etc.

crossfade looping

A sample-editing feature found in many samplers and most sample-editing software in which some portion of the data at the beginning of a loop is mixed with some portion of the data at the end of the same loop in order to produce a smoother transition between the end and the beginning of the loop.

crossover frequency

1. The frequency that is the outer limit of one of the bands of a crossover. 2. In the Lexicon 480L delay/reverberation effects unit, the frequency at which the bass-frequency reverb time is in effect rather than the mid-frequency reverb time.

cue

1. The signal fed back to musicians over headphones. 2. To set a tape or disc so that the intended selection will immediately play when the tape machine or player is started. 3. A location point entered into a computer controlling the playback or recording of a track or tape. 4. In MCI tape machines, a term meaning the same thing as *sync playback*, where the record head is used as a playback head for those tracks already recorded.

cut

1. One selection (song) on a pre-recorded music format. 2. A term with the same meaning as *mute* (ie to turn off a channel or a signal). 3. To reduce the gain of a particular band of frequencies with an equaliser. 4. To deny the passing of a particular band of frequencies (said of a filter).

cut-off frequency (turnover frequency)

1. The highest or lowest frequency in the pass band of a filter. 2. The highest or lowest frequency passed by an audio device. The cut-off frequency is usually considered to be the first frequency to be 3dB lower than a reference frequency in the middle of the bandwidth of the device.

cut-off rate/slope

The number of decibels that a filter reduces the signal for each octave past the filter's cut-off frequency (ie outside the pass band).

cycle

1. An alternation of a waveform that begins at a point, then passes through the zero line and ends up at a point with the same value and moving in the same direction as the starting point. 2. On a Solid State Logic console, a command that tells the console's computer to control the tape machine and make it play and replay a certain section of a tape.

D/A

Abbreviation of *digital-to-analogue converter*, a device which changes digital data numbers (digital audio signal) into discrete voltage level.

daisy chain

1. A hook-up of several devices where the audio signal has to pass through one device to reach the second device and through the second device to reach the third device. 2. In MIDI, a hook-up of MIDI devices where the MIDI signal has to pass though each device in order to reach the next device.

DAT

An abbreviation of *digital audio tape* and a standard format for recording digital audio on small, specially designed cassette tapes.

DAW

Abbreviation of *digital audio workstation*, a dedicated device that is both a recorder and mixer of digital audio.

dB

Abbreviation of the term *decibel*, a unit used to compare signal strengths.

dBm

1. Decibels of audio power present compared to one milliwatt of power in a 600-ohm load. 2. Very incorrectly and too-commonly-used term designating the reference voltage of .775 volts of audio signal strength, regardless of impedance.

dBSPL

The sound-pressure level present compared in decibels to the standard sound-pressure reference level representing 'no' sound (ie a sound-pressure level that about 50 per cent of people would say that they couldn't hear).

dBu (dBv)

The audio voltage present compared in decibels to the level of .775 volts of audio voltage in a circuit of any impedance.

DBX

A brand of noise reduction systems, dynamic processing equipment and other audio gear.

dead

1. An acoustically absorbent area or space. 2. A slang term for 'broken'.

decay

1. The rate of reduction of an audio signal generated in synthesisers from the peak level to the sustain level. (See also *ADSR*.) 2. The fade-out of the reverberation of a sound.

decibel

A unit of measurement used to indicate audio power level. Technically, a decibel is a logarithmic ratio of two numbers, which means that there is no such thing as a decibel measurement of a single signal. In order to measure a signal in decibels, you need to know what level it's referenced to. Commonly used reference levels are indicated by such symbols as dBm, dBV and dBu.

de-esser

1. The control circuit of an audio compressor or limiter that is made more sensitive to the sounds

made by a person pronouncing the letter S. 2. Any device that will reduce the high-frequency energy present when the letter S is pronounced loudly.

definition

1. The quality of a sound that allows it to be distinguished from other sounds. 2. In Lexicon reverb units, a parameter that sets a decrease in reverberation density in the later part of the decay.

delay

A signal that comes from a source and is then delayed by a tape machine or delay device and can then be mixed with the original (non-delayed) signal to make it sound fuller, create echo effects, etc. 1. The first stage of a five-stage DADSR envelope, which delays the beginning of the envelope's attack segment. 2. A control function that allows one of the elements in a layered sound to start later than another element. 3. A signal processor used for flanging, doubling and echo which holds its input for a period of time before passing it to the output, or the algorithm within a signal processor that creates delay.

delay effects

Any signal processing that uses delay as its basis for processing, such as echo, reverb delay and special effects, such as flanging and chorusing.

demo

1. A cheaply-made recording that gives an idea of some of the musical performances that could be used in a final music production. 2. To make a demo. 3. Any demonstration or trial use of equipment that may be purchased in the future. 4. The equipment being demonstrated.

detune

1. A control that allows one oscillator to sound a slightly different pitch than another. 2. To change the pitch of one oscillator relative to another in order to produce a fuller sound.

DI

Abbreviation of *direct injection* or *direct input*.

diaphragm

The part of the mic which moves in response to fluctuations in the sound-pressure wave.

digital

Literally 'of numbers'. Digital music equipment uses microprocessors to store, retrieve and manipulate information about sound in the form of numbers, and typically divides potentially continuous fluctuations in value – such as amplitude or pitch – into discrete quantized steps.

digital delay

A delay line or delay effects unit that converts audio signal into digital audio signal, delays it and then converts it back to analogue audio signal before sending it out of the unit.

digital interface format (DIF)

A specification of the number of bits, their meaning, the voltage and the type of connector used with digital audio connections.

digital recording

The process of converting audio signals into numbers representing the waveform and then storing these numbers.

digital signal processing (DSP)

Any signal processing done after an analogue audio signal has been converted into digital audio.

digital-to-analogue converter (DAC)

A device that changes the sample words put out by a digital audio device into analogue fluctuations in voltage that can be sent to a mixer or amplifier. All digital synthesisers, samplers and effects devices have DACs (pronounced to rhyme with fax) at their outputs to create audio signals.

dip

To reduce the levels of signals in a specific band of audio frequencies.

direct

1. Using a direct pick-up. 2. Using a direct output. 3. Recording all musicians to the final two-track master without using a multitrack tape.

direct box

An electronic device utilising a transformer or amplifier to change the electrical output of an electric instrument (for example, an electric guitar) to the impedance and level usually obtained from a microphone.

directional pattern

1. In mics, the same as *pick-up pattern*, ie a description or graphic display of the level that a mic puts out in response to sounds arriving from different directions. 2. In speakers, the pattern of dispersion (the area that the sound from a speaker will cover evenly in a listening area).

direct input

The same as *direct pick-up or DI*, ie to feed the signal from an electrical output of an electric instrument to a recording console or tape recorder without using a microphone but instead by changing the electrical output of the instrument to the same impedance and level as a mic.

direct pick-up

Feeding the signal from an electrical instrument to the recording console or tape recorder without using a microphone.

distant miking

The technique of placing a mic far from a sound source so that reflected sound is picked up with the direct sound.

distortion

1. The audio garble that can be heard when an audio waveform has been altered, usually by the overloading of an audio device like an amplifier. 2. The similar garbled sound that can be heard when the sound-pressure level is too loud for the waveform to be accurately reproduced by the human hearing mechanism.

Dolby

The name and trademark of a manufacturer of noise-reduction systems and other audio systems. These systems improve the performance and fidelity of devices that record, play back and transmit audio material.

Doppler effect

A change in frequency of a delayed signal caused by changes in the delay time while the cycle is being formed.

double

1. To record a second performance, ie double-tracking (recording a second track with a second performance closely matching the first). 2. To use a delay line with medium delay to simulate this.

drum machine

A sample playback unit or sound module with drum sounds that can be sequenced by an internal sequencer to play drum patterns.

drum pattern

A sequence of drum sounds played by a drummer or sequenced into a drum machine, especially a short pattern used in part of a song.

dry signal

A signal consisting entirely of the original, unprocessed sound. The output of an effects device is 100 per cent dry when only the input signal is being heard, ie with none of the effects created by the processor itself, with no reverberation or ambience. The term is more loosely used to describe an audio signal free of signal processing.

DSP

Abbreviation of *digital signal processing*, ie any signal processing performed after an analogue audio signal has been convened into digital audio. Broadly speaking, all changes in sound that are produced within a digital audio device - other than those caused by the simple cutting and pasting of sections of a waveform - are created via DSP. A digital reverb is a typical DSP device.

dub

1. To copy a recording. 2. A copy of a recording. 3. A recording made in time with another recording so that the final result is a combination of the first recording and the second recording. 4. To add dialogue to a picture after the picture has been filmed or recorded on videotape.

dynamic microphone

1. A microphone in which the diaphragm moves a coil suspended in a magnetic field in order to generate an output voltage proportional to the sound-pressure level. 2. Occasionally used to mean any microphone that has a generating element which cuts magnetic lines of force in order to produce an output, such as a dynamic microphone (definition 1) or a ribbon mic.

dynamic range

1. The level difference (in decibels) between the loudest peak and the softest level of a recording, etc. 2. The level difference between the level of clipping and the noise level in an audio device or channel.

dynamics

1. The amount of fluctuation in level of an audio signal. 2. In music, the playing of instruments loudly or softly.

dynamic voice allocation

A system found on many multitimbral synthesisers and samplers that allows voice channels to be reassigned automatically to play different notes (often with different sounds) whenever required by the musical input from the keyboard or MIDI.

early reflections

1. The first echoes in a room, caused by the sound from the sound source reflecting off one surface before reaching the listener. 2. A reverb algorithm whose output consists of a number of closely spaced, discrete echoes, designed to mimic the bouncing of sound off nearby walls in an acoustic space.

earth

The British version of the American term *ground* (in electronics, a place that has zero volts).

echo

1. One distinct repeat of a sound caused by the sound reflecting off a surface. 2. Loosely used to mean reverberation (ie the continuing of a sound after the source stops emitting it, caused by many discrete echoes closely spaced in time).

echo chamber

1. A room designed with very hard, non-parallel surfaces and equipped with a speaker and microphone. 2. Any artificial or electronic device that simulates the reverberation created in a room.

echo return

An input of the console which brings back the echo (reverberation) signal from the echo chamber or other echo effects device.

echo send

The output of a console used to send a signal to an echo chamber or delay effects device.

editing

1. Changing the sequence of a recording by cutting the recording tape and putting the pieces together in the new sequence with splicing tape. 2. Punching in and then punching out on one or more tracks of a multitrack tape recorder to replace previously recorded performances. 3. Changing the sequence of a digital recording's playback by using a computer program.

effects

1. An effect is a device that modifies an audio signal by adding something to the signal to change the sound. 2. Short for the term *sound effects* (sounds other than dialogue, narration or music added to film or video shots, such as door slams, wind, etc).

effects track

1. In film production, a recording of the mixdown of all of the sound effects for the film ready to be mixed with the dialogue and music. 2. In music recording, one track with a recording of effects to be added to another track of a multitrack recording.

electret condenser

A condenser microphone that has a permanently polarised (charged) variable capacitor as its sound-pressure-level sensor.

engineer

1. A technician in charge of a recording session, also called the *recording engineer*. 2. A person with an engineering degree. 3. A person with sufficient experience in the field to be equivalent to the education one would receive on an engineering degree course.

envelope

1. Description of the way in which a sound or audio signal varies in intensity over time. 2. How a control voltage changes in level over time, controlling a parameter of something other than gain or audio level. The shape of a synthesiser's envelope is controlled by a set of rate (or time) and level parameters. The envelope is a control signal that can be applied to various aspects of a synth sound, such as pitch, filter cut-off frequency and overall amplitude. Usually, each note has its own envelope(s).

envelope generator

A device that generates an envelope. Also known as a *contour generator* or *transient generator*, because the envelope is a contour (shape) that is used to create some of the transient (changing) characteristics of the sound. (See *ADSR*.)

envelope tracking

Also called *keyboard tracking*, *key follow* or *keyboard rate scaling*. A function that changes the length of one or more envelope segments, depending on which key on the keyboard is being pressed. Envelope tracking is most often used to give the higher notes shorter envelopes and the lower notes longer envelopes, mimicking the response characteristics of percussion-activated acoustic instruments, such as guitar and marimba.

equal loudness contours

A drawing of several curves showing how loud the tones of different frequencies would have to be played for it to be said that they were of equal loudness.

equalisation

Any time that the amplitudes of audio signals at specific set of frequencies are increased or decreased more than the signals at other audio frequencies.

error concealment

Replacing information in a digital audio signal to replace bits that are lost when the digital recording or processing system cannot verify whether the lost bits were ones or zeros but can make a good guess by comparing the known bits that were close in position to the lost bits.

expansion

The opposite of compression. For example, an expander may allow the signal to increase 2dB every time the signal input increases by 1dB.

fade

1. A gradual reduction of the level of an audio signal. 2. A gradual change of level from one preset level to another.

fader

A device to control the gain of a channel on a console, thereby determining the level of a signal in that channel.

far field

The area covering the distance from three feet away from the sound source up to the critical distance.

fat

Having more than a normal amount of signal strength at low frequencies or having more sound than normal by the use of compression or delay.

feed

To send an audio or control signal to a device.

feedback

1. The delayed signal sent back to the input of a delay line, used in repeat-echo effects. 2. The pick-up of the signal out of a channel by its input or the howling sound that this produces. 3. In an amplifier, the phase-reversed output signal sent back to its input, reducing gain but also causing distortion and noise.

fidelity

The recording or reproduction quality of an audio device.

figure-of-eight pattern

Another name for a bi-directional pattern, a microphone design that picks up best from the front and rear of the diaphragm and not at all from the side of the diaphragm.

filter

1. A device that removes signals with frequencies above or below a certain point, known as the *cut-off frequency*. 2. An equaliser section, used in this sense because filters are used with other components to give an equaliser its frequency response characteristics. 3. The action of removing signals of some frequencies and leaving the rest. 4. A mechanical device that smoothes out speed variations in tape machines, known as a *scrape flutter filter* or, more usually, a *scrape flutter idler*.

final mix

A two-track stereo master tape mixed from the multitrack master.

FireWire

The popular name for a high-speed digital standard connection for linking up peripherals such as digital video cameras, audio components and computer devices. FireWire was originally developed by Apple Computers as a replacement for the SCSI bus. IEEE 1394 is formal name for the standard. Vendors must obtain a licence from Apple in order to use the term FireWire.

flange

An effect caused by combining an approximately even mix of a modulated (varying) short delay with the direct signal.

flat

1. Lower in musical pitch. 2. A slang term used to describe the sensitivity to frequency of a microphone, amplifier, etc, as being even at all frequencies (usually within 2dB).

Fletcher Munson effect

A hearing limitation shown by Fletcher Munson equal-loudness contours that, as music is lowered in volume, it's much more difficult to hear bass frequencies and somewhat harder to hear very high frequencies.

floor

1. An alternative term to *range* (ie a limit on the amount that a signal is reduced when the input signal is lowered by an expander or gate). 2. A shortening of the term *noise floor* (ie the level of noise).

flutter

1. High-frequency variations in pitch of a recorded waveform due to rapid variations in speed of a recorder or playback machine. 2. Originally, and more formally, any variations - fast or slow - in the pitch of a recorded tone due to speed fluctuations in a recorder or playback unit.

fly in

1. To add sounds into a mix or recording that have no synchronisation. 2. An application of this is where a performance from one part of a tune is recorded and then recorded back into the recording at a different time in the recording.

foldback

A European term for the signal sent to the stage monitors in a live performance.

formant

An element in the sound of a voice or instrument that doesn't change frequency as different pitches are sounded. Can also be described as a resonant peak in a frequency spectrum. The variable formants produced by the human vocal tract are what give vowels their characteristic sound.

frequency

The number of cycles of a waveform occurring in the space of a second.

frequency range

The range of frequencies over which an electronic device is useful or over which a sound source puts out substantial energy.

frequency response

The measure of sensitivity shown by an electronic device (microphone, amplifier, speaker, etc) to various frequencies. Often communicated via a graph.

full step

A change in pitch that occurs when one moves up or down two piano keys.

gain

An increase in the strength of an audio signal, often expressed in decibels.

gain control

A device that changes the gain of an amplifier or circuit. Often appears as a knob that can be turned or a slider that can be moved up and down.

gain reduction

A reduction in gain during high-level passages, effected by a limiter or compressor.

gain structure

The way in which gain changes at the various stages or sections of an audio system.

gate

A dynamics-processing device that turns a channel off or down when a signal drops below a certain level.

General MIDI (GM)

A set of requirements adopted by manufacturers of MIDI devices and used to ensure the consistent playback performance on all instruments bearing the GM logo. Some of the requirements include 24-voice polyphony and a standardised group of sounds and their locations. For example, patch 17 will always be a drawbar organ sound on all General MIDI instruments.

generating element

The portion of a microphone that actually converts the movement of the diaphragm into electrical current or changes in voltage.

glide

A function where the pitch slides smoothly from one note to the next instead of jumping over the intervening pitches. Also called *portamento*.

golden section

A ratio of exact height to width to length of a room in order to achieve good acoustics. First recommended by the ancient Greeks. The ratio is approximately the width of a room x 1.6 times its height and its length x 2.6 times its height.

gigabyte

One billion bytes.

global

Pertaining to or governing all of the operations of an instrument.

graphic editing

A method of editing parameter values using graphical representations (for example, of envelope shapes) displayed on a computer screen or LCD.

graphic equaliser

A device equipped with several slides to control the gain of an audio signal present within one of several evenly spaced frequency bands, spaced according to octaves.

ground

US equivalent of British *earth*. In electronics, a place (terminal) that has zero volts.

group

1. A number of channels or faders that can be controlled by one master VCA slide. 2. A shortening of the term *recording group* (ie a bus or the signal present on a bus).

group faders

The VCA faders of a number of individual channels that are all controlled by a group master fader (ie a slide control used to send out a control voltage to several VCA faders in individual channels).

grouping

1. Controlling the gain of several individual channels with a group fader. 2. The mixing together of several individual audio signals to send a mixed signal out of the console to record a track on a multitrack tape machine.

group master

A slide control used to send out a control voltage to several VCA faders in individual channels, thus controlling the gain of several channels.

guitar controller

An electric guitar or device played like an electric guitar that produces MIDI signals which can be used to control synthesisers and sound modules.

guitar processor

A unit that adds effects to a direct guitar signal, including a simulated instrument amplifier sound and, often, delay and reverb effects.

Haas effect

Simply stated, a factor in human hearing where delay has a much bigger effect on the human perception of direction than level does.

half step

A difference in pitch present between adjacent keys on a piano.

hall program

A setting of a digital delay/reverb effects unit that approximates concert halls. Hall programs are characterised by a pre-delay of up to 25ms.

harmonic

A frequency that is a whole-number multiple of the fundamental frequency. For example, if the fundamental frequency of a sound is 440Hz, the first two harmonics are 880Hz and 1,320Hz (1.32kHz). Harmonics are whole-number multiples of the frequency that determines the timbre recognition of an instrument's sound.

harmonic distortion

The presence of harmonics in the output signal of a device that weren't present in the input signal.

headphones

Devices that can be worn on the head fitted with small speakers that fit over the ears or, sometimes, into the ears.

headroom

1. The level difference (in decibels) between normal operating level and clipping level in an amplifier or audio device. 2. A similar level difference between normal tape-operating level and the level at which the distortion would be 3 per cent.

hearing limitation

An inability of the human ear to hear important characteristics of sound under certain conditions. Characteristics that can be affected include pitch, level, clarity, presence and direction.

Hertz

The basic unit of frequency, equivalent to *cycles per second*. The term is usually abbreviated to Hz.

high frequencies

Audio frequencies at 6,000Hz and above.

high impedance

Impedance of 5,000 ohms or more.

high-impedance mic

A microphone designed to be fed into an amplifier with an input impedance greater than 20,000 ohms.

high-pass filter

A device that rejects signals below a certain frequency (known as the *cut-off frequency*) and passes signals with frequencies that are higher than this.

highs

Abbreviation of *high frequencies* (ie audio frequencies of 6,000Hz and higher).

hypercardioid pattern

A microphone pick-up sensitivity pattern demonstrating that the least-sensitive pick-up point is more than 90 degrees but less than 150 degrees off axis (usually 120 degrees).

Hz

Abbreviation of *Hertz*, the unit of frequency.

IM distortion

Abbreviation of *intermodulation distortion*, which is caused by one signal beating with another signal and producing frequencies that are both the sum and the difference of the original frequencies present.

impedance

The opposition to alternating current (AC).

impedance matching

Having or converting the output impedance of a device so that it matches the impedance of the input that it will feed.

infinite repeat

A function on some delay lines that cause enough feedback for the repeat echo to last forever but not enough to cause a howling sound.

in port

A jack on a MIDI device or computer that will accept an incoming data signal.

input

1. The jack or physical location of the point at which a device receives a signal. 2. A signal being received by a device. 3. To feed a signal from one device to another.

input/output module

A set of controls on one housing for an in-line console that has two channels – one for recording and one for monitoring – and which has controls for all console sections.

insert

1. A punch in performed on all of the tracks being recorded in a recording session. 2. On Solid State Logic consoles, to place an outboard piece of gear in a channel by patching and activating a switch.

interface

Any device that allows one unit to work, drive or communicate with another unit when they can't do so by just feeding each other, often because the units are manufactured by different companies.

intermodulation distortion

Form of distortion caused by one signal beating with another signal and producing frequencies that are both the sum and the difference of the original frequencies.

inverse square law

This expresses the fact that, in an unobstructed area (such as an open field), the sound-pressure level will drop to half pressure (-6dB) every time the distance to a sound source is doubled.

I/O

Abbreviation of *input/output,* referring to: 1. an in-line console module that contains controls for the input section, output section and monitor section; 2. a module in electronic gear containing input and output amplifiers for the device; and 3. a digital port (connector) able to both receive digital data and output digital data.

isolation

A containing of the sound wave in a certain area so that it won't leak into other areas and/or unintended mics.

isolation booth/room

A room that prevents loud sounds produced by other instruments from leaking in.

jack

A connector mounted on the casing of a device or on a panel.

jack bay

A series of jacks that have connections for most of the inputs and outputs of the equipment in a control room.

jam sync

A generation of new SMPTE according to the input SMPTE signal.

key

The control of a dynamics-processing device via an external audio signal.

keyboard

1. Any musical instrument controlled by pressing a key. 2. The part of the computer that has the keys.

keyboard controller

A device that has the standard music keys of piano but transmits MIDI signals.

keyboard scaling

A function by which the sound can be altered smoothly across the range of a keyboard by using key numbers as a modulation source. Level scaling changes the loudness of the sound, while filter scaling changes its brightness.

keying input/key input

An input on a dynamics-processing device used to control the device via an external audio signal.

key note number

A number assigned to each key of a synthesiser or controller keyboard that is transmitted in the MIDI signal.

kHz

Abbreviation of *kiloHertz* (1,000 Hertz).

kilobyte (KB)

Linguistically, 1,000 bytes. In practice, a kilobyte generally contains 1,024 bytes.

layering

The recording or playing of a musical part with several similar sound patches playing simultaneously.

lead

The musical instrument or vocal that plays or sings the melody of a tune.

lead sheet

A written chart showing the melody, lyrics and chords of a tune, complete with full musical notation.

leakage

Sounds from other instruments and sources that weren't intended to be picked up by a microphone.

level

The amount of signal strength (ie the amplitude, especially the average amplitude).

lift

To boost the gain of an audio signal at a particular band of frequencies with an equaliser.

limiter

A device that reduces gain when the input voltage exceeds a certain level.

line level

An amplified signal level put out by an amplifier and used as the normal level that runs through the interconnecting cables in a control room.

line out(put)

Any output that sends out a line-level signal, such as the output of a console that feeds a recorder.

link

A term used with reference to compressors and dynamic-processing units meaning to combine the control input signals of two channels of a compressor (or dynamic-processing unit) so that both channels always have the same gain and are triggered to change gain by the signal of either channel.

listen circuits

A type of solo circuit that allows you to listen to a channel before the fader or after the fader.

live

1. Refers to the sound produced by instruments during a performance to an audience. 2. Having a large portion of reverberant or reflected sound.

live recording

1. The practice of recording where all musicians are playing at once and no overdubbing takes place. 2. Recorded material with a lot of natural reverberation.

load impedance

The opposition to the flow of output current caused by the input that it feeds.

Local (mode) On/Off

A switch or function in a synthesiser that connects (On) or disconnects (Off) the keyboard control of the synthesiser's sound module.

long delay

Delay times greater than 60ms.

loop

1. The same as *anti-node*, ie the points of maximum displacement of motion in a vibrating, stretched string. 2. A piece of material that plays over and over. In a sequencer, a loop repeats a musical phrase. In a sampler, loops are used to allow samples of finite length to be sustained indefinitely.

loudness control

A knob that changes the level and adjusts the frequency response of the circuit controlling the speakers in order to compensate for the inability of the ear to hear low frequencies and extremely high frequencies at low volumes.

low end

A slang term for bass-frequency signals (ie those below 250Hz).

lower toms

Large toms that sit on the floor, mounted on metal feet, with heads up to approximately 20 inches in diameter.

low frequencies

1. Audio or audible frequencies below 1kHz. 2. The range of bass frequencies below approximately 250Hz.

low-frequency oscillator

An oscillator that puts out an AC signal between .1Hz and 10Hz, used for a control signal. Especially devoted to applications below the audible frequency range, and typically used as a control source for modulating a sound to create vibrato, tremolo, trills and so on.

low impedance

Impedance of 500 ohms or less.

low-pass filter

A device that rejects signals above a certain frequency and passes those that are lower in frequency.

map

A table in which input values are arbitrarily assigned to outputs by the user on an item-by-item basis.

mapper

A device that translates MIDI data from one form to another in real time.

margin

The amount of decibels between the highest peak level of a program and the point at which overload occurs.

masking

The characteristic of hearing by which loud sounds prevent the ear from hearing softer sounds of similar frequency.

master

1. A control to set the level going out of a console, especially the stereo output to a two-track machine at mixdown. 2. A term with the same meaning as *sub-master*, ie a control that adjusts the level of a signal mixed together and sent out to one track of a multitrack recorder. 3. A term with the same meaning as *VCA master*, ie one slider that controls the

control voltage sent to several VCA faders. 4. A machine used as a speed reference when synchronising two or more machines to run together. If the master tape transport changes speed, the other machines synced to it will change speed with it. 5. The original recording, used for making copies. 6. To make an original recording which will be used to make commercial copies, especially making a master lacquer (for record manufacturing) or a master CD.

master fader

1. The fader which controls the main output(s) of a console during mixdown. 2. In some consoles, faders which control outputs to a multitrack tape recorder during recording. 3. Occasionally used to mean a VCA master (ie one slide that controls the control voltage sent to several VCA faders).

MCI

Abbreviation of *media control interface*, a multimedia specification designed to provide control of onscreen movies and peripherals, such as CD-ROM drives.

MDM

Abbreviation of the term *modular digital multitrack*, ie a multitrack digital recorder with (usually) eight tracks that can be run in synchronisation with other machines (of the same type) in order to attain more tracks. An example of this type of machine is the ADAT (Alesis' modular digital multitrack recording system).

measure

The grouping of a number of beats in music.

medium delay

Delay times of 20-60ms.

meg(a)

1. A prefix for 1,000,000. 2. A slang abbreviation of megaHertz (1,000,000Hz) or megabytes (1,024,000 bytes).

merger

A MIDI accessory that allows two incoming MIDI signals to be combined into one MIDI output.

meter

A device which measures or compares electrical signals, often used to read the voltage levels of audio signals.

mic

Abbreviation of *microphone*.

mic gain control

A level control on a mic pre-amp that sets gain and is used to prevent the overload of that pre-amp.

mic input

The input of a console or other device into which a microphone can be plugged.

mic level

The very low audio voltage level that comes out of a studio microphone.

mic/line switch

The selector switch on the input of a console channel that chooses which input jack feeds the console.

mic pad

A device that reduces the level of a signal, placed just before a microphone pre-amplifier to prevent overloading of the pre-amplifier.

mic pre-amp

An amplifier that boosts the low-level audio signal produced by a microphone up to line level.

MIDI

Abbreviation of *musical instrument digital interface*, a digital signal system (ie a system of number signals) used to send and receive performance information to and from musical instruments.

MIDI channel

A grouping of data concerning the performance of one synthesiser or device separate from the data concerning other synthesisers or devices. MIDI commands contain all of the information that a sound board needs to reproduce the desired sound.

MIDI clock

Time data in a MIDI signal that advances one step each $1/24$ of a beat and can be used to sync two sequencers together.

MIDI clock with song pointer

A MIDI clock that which also has a number signal for each measure or bar to indicate the number of measures or bars into the tune.

MIDI controller

A device that can be played by a musician that transmits MIDI signals to control synthesisers or sound modules.

MIDI echo

A function in a synthesiser that causes the output of a sequencer to send a MIDI signal out of the out port matching the MIDI signal coming in for the track being recorded.

MIDI interface

A device that converts a MIDI signal into the digital format used by a computer so that the computer can store and use the MIDI signal.

MIDI mode

Any of the ways in which devices respond to incoming MIDI data. While four modes – Omni Off/Poly, Omni On/Poly, Omni Off/Mono and Omni On/Mono – are defined by the MIDI specification, Omni On/Mono is never used. There are also at least two other useful modes that have been developed: Multi mode, for multitimbral instruments, and Multi-Mono mode, for guitar synthesisers.

MIDI patch bay

A device that has several MIDI inputs and outputs and allows any input to be routed to any output.

MIDI sample dump

The copying of a digitally recorded sample without converting it to analogue between different storage units or sound modules through a MIDI transmission.

MIDI sequencer

A computer that can record and play back MIDI data in such a way as to control the performance of MIDI-controlled musical instruments or devices in a series of timed steps.

MIDI Thru

There are two types of MIDI Thru. One, a simple hardware connection, is found on the back panels of many synthesisers. This Thru jack simply duplicates whatever data is arriving at the MIDI In jack. Sequencers have a second type, called Software Thru, where data arriving at the In jack is merged with data being played by the sequencer, and both sets of data appear in a single stream at the Out (rather than the Thru) jack. Software Thru is useful because it allows you to hook a master keyboard to the sequencer's MIDI In and a tone module to its Out. You can then play the keyboard and hear the tone module, and the sequencer can also send its messages directly to the tone module.

MIDI time code

All of the information contained in SMPTE time code that has been converted into part of the MIDI signal.

mid-range frequencies

Audio frequencies from around 250Hz through to 6,000Hz.

MiniDisc

A small, recordable compact disc that can be used by general consumers, introduced by Sony at the end of 1992.

mix

1. To blend audio signals together into a composite signal. 2. The signal made by blending individual signals together. 3. A control or function on a delay/reverberation device that controls the amount of direct signal that is mixed into the processed signal.

mixer

1. A console or other device that blends audio signals into composite signals and has a small number of outputs. 2. A section on a console that performs this function. 3. In Europe, a fader. 4. An engineer or technician who mixes, especially a live-sound mix during a live performance.

mixing console/desk

A device that can combine several signals into one or more composite signals in any proportion.

mixing solo

A button that turns off all other channels, thus allowing the signal to be heard in the stereo perspective and the level used at mixdown, and with reverberation also applied.

modulation

The control of one signal by another AC signal.

modulation noise

Noise that is present only when the audio signal is present.

monitor

1. To listen, in the context of audio. 2. To indicate with a meter or light the conditions in a circuit, especially level and overload. 3. A device designed to listen or observe.

monitor mixer

1. A console or other device that blends audio signals into composite signals and has a small number of outputs. 2. The section of a console that is used to complete a rough mix so that an engineer can hear what's being recorded without effecting the levels being fed to the multitrack recorder. 3. The audio technician who mixes the signals sent to the stage monitor speakers.

monitor pot

A rotary control used to set the level of the track signal in the monitor (ie the signal to or the signal back from one track of a multitrack tape recorder).

monitor (mixer) section

The section of a console that is used to complete a rough mix so that an engineer can hear what's being recorded without effecting the levels being fed to the multitrack recorder.

monitor selector

1. On consoles, a switch that allows you to hear various things over the control-room monitor speakers, such as the main console outputs (for mixing purposes), the monitor mixer section (for recording and overdubbing), the disc player, tape machines and other devices. 2. On tape machines, a switch that, in one position, sends the signal from the tape to the meters and the output of the machine's electronics or, in a second position, sends the input signal being fed to the machine to the meters and the outputs of the electronic devices.

monophonic/mono

1. More formal term for mono and meaning that there is only one sound source, or that the signal was derived from one sound source. 2. In synthesisers, a term meaning that only one pitch may be sounded at a time.

moving-coil microphone

The same as *dynamic microphone*, ie a mic in which the diaphragm moves a coil suspended in a magnetic field in order to generate an output voltage proportional to the sound-pressure level.

moving-fader automation

In consoles, a feature that enables an engineer to program changes in fader levels so that these changes happen automatically upon playback of a multitrack recording, because the fader positions actually change. The faders are driven by tiny motors.

MP3

Abbreviation of MPEG 1, audio layer 3. MPEG stands for Moving Picture Experts Group, and is used to describe a number of file-compression formats used for audio and video files. The idea of MP3 is that it disregards repeated information and also ignores any fluctuations or inaudible harmonics. OK, it's a bit more complicated than that, but you get the idea. Despite the current hype, MP3 doesn't really deliver sound quality that's even close to that of CD or even MiniDisc, but it does create relatively small files (ie around a tenth of the size of normal audio files).

MS miking

A method of placing stereo microphones so that one cardioid microphone points directly at the middle of the area to be miked and a bi-directional microphone is as close as possible to the first mic, with its rejection pointing the same way as the axis of the first mic.

MTC

Abbreviation of *MIDI time code*, ie all of the information of SMPTE time code that has been converted into part of the MIDI signal.

Multi mode

A MIDI reception mode in which a multitimbral module responds to MIDI input on two or more channels and maintains musical independence between the channels, typically playing a different patch on each channel.

multisample

The distribution of several related samples at different pitches across a keyboard. Multisampling can provide greater realism in sample playback (wavetable) synthesis, since the individual samples don't have to be transposed over a great distance.

multitimbral

A synthesiser that is able to send out several signals of different sound patches (and often playing different parts) or has several sound modules is said to be multitimbral.

multitrack recording

1. Recording various instruments separately on different portions of the same tape in time with each other so that final balancing of the sound may be accomplished later. 2. Digitally recording various instruments onto a hard disk in different data files so that they may be played in time with each other and so that the final balancing of the sound may be accomplished later.

Mute switch

A switch that turns off a channel, takes out a track signal from the monitors or turns off the entire monitor signal.

near field

The area up to one foot away from the sound source.

negative feedback

Used to describe an out-of-phase portion of an output signal fed into the input of an amplifier.

noise

1. Random energy that contains energy at all audio frequencies. 2. Any unintentional or objectionable signal added to an audio signal.

noise filter

A filter that passes only signals with the intended audio frequencies, thus eliminating noise signals at other frequencies.

noise floor

The level of noise below the signal, measured in decibels.

noise gate

A gate used to turn off an audio channel when noise but no signal is present.

noise reduction

Any device designed to remove noise in a device or system.

non-directional

Used with microphones to mean the same thing as *omni-directional* (ie picking up sound from all directions).

normalize

1. To provide normalized switches on a jack. 2. To reset a synthesiser, sound module or sample-playback unit to the original factory settings. 3. To adjust the level of a selection so that the highest peak is at the maximum recording level of the medium. 4. To boost the level of a waveform to its maximum amount without experiencing clipping (distortion), thus maximising resolution and minimising certain types of noise.

Nyquist frequency

The highest frequency that can be recorded and reproduced properly by a particular sampling rate. Theoretically, the Nyquist frequency is half of the sampling rate. For example, when a digital recording uses a sampling rate of 44.1kHz, the Nyquist frequency is 22.05kHz. If a signal being sampled contains frequency components that are above the Nyquist frequency, aliasing will be introduced in the digital representation of the signal, unless those frequencies are filtered out prior to digital encoding.

Nyquist rate

The lowest sampling rate that can be used to record and reproduce a given audio frequency.

octave

A difference of pitch where one tone has a frequency that is double or half that of another tone.

off axis

1. Away from the front or axis of the mic. Measured in degrees. 2. 180 degrees from the front.

offset/offset time

1. SMPTE time that triggers a MIDI sequencer. 2. The amount of position difference needed to get two reels to play music in time.

omni-directional

1. Used to describe microphones that pick up evenly from all directions. 2. Used to describe speakers that send out evenly in all directions.

Omni mode

When Omni mode is activated in a MIDI device, all MIDI messages are recognising and acted on, no matter what their channel.

OMS

Abbreviation of *open music system* (formerly *Opcode MIDI system*), a real-time MIDI operating system for Macintosh applications. OMS allows communication between different MIDI programs and hardware so that, for example, a sequencer could interface with a librarian program to display synthesiser patch names in the sequencer's editing windows, rather than just numbers.

on axis

The position directly in front of the diaphragm of a microphone, in line with its direction of movement.

outboard equipment

Equipment that is used with, but is not part of, a console.

out of phase

1. Being similar to another signal in amplitude, frequency and wave shape but being offset in time by part of a cycle. 2. Having the opposite polarity (ie being 180 degrees out of phase).

out port

A jack that sends out digital data from a computer or digital device.

output

1. The jack or physical location at which a device sends out a signal. 2. The signal put out by a device.

output level

The signal level at the output of a device.

overdub

To record additional parts alongside or merged with previous tracks. Overdubbing enables 'one-man band' productions, as multiple synchronised performances are recorded sequentially.

Over-Easy

DBX's trademark term for the gradual change of compression ratio around the threshold, thus making it difficult to detect when compression is taking place.

overload

To put out too much signal level, thereby causing distortion.

oversampling

A process where the analogue audio (or the digital audio, for playback) is sampled many times more than the minimum sampling rate.

overtones

The harmonics of an instrument's sound minus the fundamental frequency.

pad

1. An attenuator usually used to prevent the overloading of the amplifier that follows it. 2. A device with a surface that can be hit by a drum stick, whereby hitting the pad produces an output signal pulse (or MIDI command) which causes a drum machine or synthesiser to produce a drum sound.

pan pot

An electrical device that distributes one audio signal to two or more channels or speakers.

parameter

A user-adjustable quantity that governs an aspect of a device's performance. Normally, the settings of all of the parameters that make up a synthesiser patch can be changed by the user and stored in memory, but the parameters themselves are defined by the operating system and cannot be altered.

parametric EQ

An equaliser in which all of the parameters of equalisation can be adjusted to any amount, including centre frequency, the amount of boost or cut in gain and bandwidth.

partial

1. In acoustic instruments, a term with the same meaning as *overtone*. 2. In synthesisers, the term means literally 'part of a sound patch', ie circuitry in the synthesiser that generates and/or modifies elements of a sound in order to provide a particular tone with timbre. 3. The sound element generated by definition 2.

pass band

The frequency range of signals that will be passed by a filter, rather than the range within which signals are reduced.

patch

To connect together - as in the inputs and outputs of various modules - generally with patch cords. Also applied to the configuration of hook-ups and settings that results from the process of patching and, by extension, the sound that such a configuration creates. Often used to denote a single tone colour or the contents of a memory location that contains parameter settings for such a tone colour, even on an instrument that requires no physical patching.

patch bay

A series of jacks with connections for most of the inputs and outputs of a console, the console sections, tape machines and other pieces of equipment.

patch editor

A computer program that allows the creation or the changing of sound patch parameters, thereby creating or modifying a specific synthesised sound outside a synthesiser.

patch map

A map with which any incoming MIDI Program Change message can be assigned to call up any of an instrument's patches (sounds).

patch panel

A series of jacks with connections for most of the inputs and outputs of the console, console sections, tape machines and other pieces of equipment.

PCM

Abbreviation of *pulse-code modulation*, ie the use of amplitude pulses in magnetic tape to record the digital information bits comprising digital audio data.

peak

1. The highest point in an audio waveform. 2. Short for *peak detecting* (ie responding to a peak) or *peak indicating* (ie showing a peak). 3. Having a frequency response that would draw something similar to a mountain peak on a frequency response graph.

peak detecting

Recognising and responding to peak values of a waveform, rather than average values.

peak indicating meter

A meter that reads the absolute peak level of a waveform.

peaking filter

An EQ circuit which exhibits a peak response.

peak level

The same as *peak value*, ie the maximum positive or negative instantaneous value of a waveform.

peak-to-peak value

The difference in amplitude between positive and negative peaks. Equal to twice the peak value for a sine wave.

peak value

The maximum positive or negative instantaneous value of a waveform.

percentage quantization

A method of quantization by which notes recorded into a sequencer with uneven rhythms aren't shifted all the way to their theoretically perfect timings but are instead shifted part of the way, with the degree of shift being dependent on a user-selected percentage (quantization strength). (See *quantization*.)

phantom powering

A system used to supply condenser microphones with power, thus eliminating the need for external power supplies.

phase

A measurement (expressed in degrees) of the time difference between two similar waveforms.

phase addition

Phase addition occurs when the energy of one waveform increases the energy of another waveform because the two waveforms have similar phase relationships.

phase cancellation

Phase cancellation occurs when the energy of one waveform decreases the energy of another waveform because of phase relationships at or close to 180 degrees.

phase distortion

A change in a sound because of a phase shift in the signal.

phase-distortion synthesis

A method of altering a wave shape in order to add harmonics by phase-shifting while a cycle is being formed.

phase reversal

A change in a circuit effected in order to cause a waveform to shift by 180 degrees.

phase shift

A delay introduced into an audio signal, measured in degrees delayed.

phasing

An effect sound created by the variable phase-shifting of an audio signal mixed with the direct signal.

phon

1. A unit of equal loudness for all audio frequencies. 2. The phon is numerically equal to dBSPL (Sound-Pressure Level) at 1,000Hz but varies at other frequencies according to ear sensitivity.

phono plug

1. The same as *RCA plug*. 2. Acommon audio connector found on most stereo systems, with a centre pin as one connection and an outer shell as the second connection.

pick-up

1. A device on an electric guitar (or other instrument) that puts out an audio signal according to the motion of the strings on the instrument. 2. A device that puts out an audio signal according to the vibration of something. This term means the same thing as *contact microphone*.

pick-up pattern

The shape of the area from which a microphone will evenly pick up sound, giving similar but less detailed information than a polar pattern.

pink noise

Noise that has equal energy per octave or portion of an octave.

pitch

1. The ear's perception of frequency (ie music sounding higher or lower). 2. A control on a tape machine which increases or decreases speed slightly, thus changing the pitch and time of the music. 3. The spacing of the grooves on a phonographic record.

pitch bend

1. In a synthesiser, the pitch-bend control makes the pitch smoothly glide upwards slightly. 2. The wheel controller or MIDI command used to bring this about.

pitch change

1. A characteristic of human hearing where bass frequencies sound lower in pitch at high levels of sound pressure, often as much as 10 per cent lower. 2. A function of a delay device where the pitch of the output signal is different to that of the input signal.

pitch ratio

The percentage of pitch change in a delay line's pitch-change program.

pitch shift

To change the pitch of a sound without changing its duration, as opposed to *pitch transpose*, which changes both. Some people use the two terms interchangeably.

pitch-to-MIDI converter

A device that converts audio signals into MIDI information.

pitch-to-voltage converter

A device that converts the frequency changes of audio signals into proportional voltage changes.

plate

1. A type of reverb device in which a large metal sheet is suspended on spring clips and driven like a speaker cone. 2. An electrode in a tube that receives electrons.

plate program

A setting in a digital delay/reverb device that simulates the sound of plate reverberation.

plug-in

A software program that acts as an extension to a larger program, adding new features.

polarising voltage

Voltage applied to the plates of the variable capacitor in a condenser microphone capsule.

Pole mode

A MIDI mode that allows voices of controlled synth to be assigned polyphonically by incoming key-note numbers. The more poles a filter has, the more abrupt its cut-off slope. Each pole causes a slope of 6dB per octave. Typical configurations are two- and four-pole (12dB and 24dB per octave).

polyphonic

Used to describe a device capable of producing more than one note at a time. All synthesisers place a limit on how many voices of polyphony are available. General-MIDI-compliant synthesisers are required to provide 24 voices of polyphony.

polyphony

The number of voices (notes) that a device can produce at once.

poly(phonic) pressure

Also called key pressure. A type of MIDI channel message by which each key senses and transmits pressure data independently.

pop shield/filter

A device placed over a microphone or between the microphone and singer to prevent loud popping sounds - caused by breath on the microphone - from being picked up.

portamento

1. A pitch change that glides smoothly from one pitch to another. 2. The synthesiser mode or MIDI command that allows or causes this to happen.

ported-case microphone

A microphone with at least one port (opening behind the diaphragm) in its casing.

post-echo

The positioning of an echo send control after the main channel fader.

pot

Abbreviation of *potentiometer*, a device that outputs part of the input voltage according to the position of the control's knob.

pre-amp

A low-noise amplifier designed to take a low-level signal and bring it up to normal line level.

precedence effect

A factor in human hearing where delay has a much bigger effect on the human perception of the location of the sound source than level does.

pre-delay

Delay circuits at the input of a reverb device that produce a delay before the reverberation is heard.

pre-echo

1. A repeating of the sound before the reverberation is heard. Used to simulate reflections found in a stage environment. 2. In tape recording, a low-level leakage of sound coming later, caused by print-through (ie data leaking through onto the other side of the tape). 3. In disc recording, a similar sound caused by a groove deforming a later groove. 4. The positioning of an echo send control before the main channel fader.

pre-fader

The positioning of a send or other control before the main channel fader.

pre-fader listen

A solo circuit that allows a channel signal to be heard (and often metered) before the channel fader.

pre-mix

1. The same as *pong* (ie to play several recorded tacks with sync playback through a console in order to mix them together and record them on an open track). 2. To mix together the audio of several devices before sending the composite mix to the main console. 3. The composite mix of definitions 1 or 2.

pre-/post-switch

A switch on an input module which determines whether the echo send control comes before or after the main channel fader.

presence

The quality in an instrument (or sound source) that makes it sound like it's right there next to you.

presence frequencies

The range of audio frequencies between 4kHz and 6kHz that often, when boosted, increase the sense of presence, especially with voices.

preset

1. A sound programmed into a device at the factory by the manufacturer. 2. A factory-set parameter that gives one effect on a signal-processing device. Some manufacturers distinguish between presets, programs and patches, each of which may contain a different set of parameters.

pressure-gradient microphone

A microphone whose diaphragm that is exposed at the front and at the back and whose diaphragm movement is caused by the difference in pressure between its front and back.

pressure microphone

A microphone whose diaphragm moves because the pressure of a sound wave causes one side of the diaphragm to work against the normal or controlled air pressure inside the mic case.

pressure-operated microphone

The same as *pressure microphone*.

pressure sensitivity

The feature in a synthesiser or keyboard controller of aftertouch (a control or operational function of a synthesiser where the exerting of pressure on a key after it has been pressed, and before it is released, will activate a control command that can be set by the player).

pressure zone microphone (PZM)

Barrier microphone manufactured by Crown. The head of the mic is attached closely to a plate designed to be attached to a larger surface and which has a half-omni pick-up pattern.

preview

1. To play an edit in a digital-audio editing system before committing to save it. 2. In a computer-assisted punch in, to have the computer play over the area while switching the monitoring so that the effect of the punch in can be heard before it is performed. 3. Short for *preview signal*.

producer

The director of an audio-recording project and the person responsible for obtaining a final product of desired quality within a budget.

production

1. The recording of a tune, collection of tunes, video or film performance. 2. The action of directing an audio recording project to obtain a final product of desired quality within a budget.

program

1. The instructions, the action of instructing or the action of recording instructions for a

computer or computer-controlled device in order to compel it to perform certain functions. 2. A sound patch, ie the sequence of tone generators and modifiers in a synthesiser designed to obtain a particular sound. 3. The settings (especially those set at the factory) that will obtain a certain effect in an effects processor. 4. One selection of recorded music on a CD or DAT. 5. The audio that is recorded in general.

program change

A MIDI message sent to a receiving device that will change its presets, causing a synthesiser or other device to switch to a new program (also called a preset or patch) contained in its memory.

program equalisation

Changing the level of any signal in a certain range of frequencies to emphasise or de-emphasise certain elements in the frequency of an instrument or sound source and change its tone.

program time

In DAT recording, the time indication from the top of one selection.

proprietary

Describing a function, feature or characteristic owned by one company and available only in units manufactured by that company.

protocol

A system of digital data where the positioning of the data, and the significance of each bit in the data stream, is determined according to a standardised format so that all devices can properly interpret the data.

proximity effect

In directional microphones, this is the boost in the microphone's output for bass frequencies as the mic is moved closer to the sound source.

psychoacoustics

The study of how things sound to individuals because of mental, emotional or other personal factors.

pulse

A rise and then fall in amplitude, similar to a square wave, but one which stays up for less time than it stays down.

pulse-code modulation

The use of amplitude pulses in magnetic tape to record the digital information bits of digital audio.

pulse-wave modulation

Moving smoothly from a square wave to a pulse wave, in response to a control-voltage input (usually from a LFO).

pulse width

The amount of time that a pulse is at maximum voltage.

punching in

Putting a recorder/sequencer in Record mode on a previously-recorded track while the track is playing in Sync Playback mode and the singer or musician is singing or playing along.

pure tone

A tone without harmonic frequencies (except for the fundamental frequency) and with a sine-wave shape.

PZM

A trademark belonging to Crown for its barrier microphone. (See *pressure zone microphone.*)

Q

The sharpness of the peak response in an equalisation circuit.

quality factor

The ratio of reactance to resistance in a coil which affects Q.

quantization distortion error

A modulation noise (also perceived as a distortion) that occurs in digital processing and recording and is caused by the sample levels being altered to conform to standard quantization levels.

quantization/quantizing levels/increments

A standard level that can be recognised by a digital recording system.

quantization noise

A modulation noise (also perceived as distortion) that occurs in digital processing and recording and is caused by the sample levels being altered to conform to standard quantization levels. This is one of the types of error introduced into an analogue audio signal by encoding it in digital form. The digital equivalent of tape hiss, quantization noise is caused by the small differences between the actual amplitudes of the points being sampled and the bit resolution of the analogue-to-digital converter.

quantize

The conversion of the values of an analogue wave or random occurrence into steps. Quantizing is a function found on sequencers and drum machines and causes notes played at odd times to be 'rounded off' to regular rhythmic values.

rack

1. The physical setting of a head in the direction toward or away from the tape, therefore affecting how much pressure is applied on the head by the tape. 2. Short for *equipment rack*, a cabinet with rails, or free-standing rails, that have holes in them to accept screws at standard spaces. Used to house outboard gear.

ramp wave

A waveform that is similar to a sawtooth waveform but differs in that it starts at zero level and gradually rises to its peak level and then instantly drops back to zero level to form one cycle.

random-note generator

A device that generates unpredictable pitches at a set rate. Used in synthesisers.

random phase

The presence of many signals or reflections where some of the signals are in phase and some out of phase. The overall effect is that of being between in phase and out of phase.

rap

To perform a spoken rhythmic part to a music or percussion performance. Considered by some to be people talking bollocks.

real time

Occurring at the same time as other, usually human, activities. In real-time sequence recording, timing information is encoded, along with the note data, as the computer analyses the timing of the input. In real-time editing, changes in parameter settings can be heard immediately, without the need to play a new note or wait for computational processes to be completed.

reconstruction filter

A low-pass filter on the output of a digital-to-analogue converter that smoothes the staircase-like changes in voltage produced by the converter in order to eliminate clock noise from the output.

recording session

Any period where music is being recorded, especially the first such period, where the rhythm instruments are being recorded.

recording solo

A switch or function which routes the signal of a channel to the monitor system by itself, and yet the signals out of the console to the recorder are uninterrupted.

reflected sound

Sound that reaches a mic or listener after reflecting once or more from surrounding surfaces.

release

1. The rate at which the volume of a synthesiser drops to silence once a key is released. 2. The portion of an envelope that begins after a key is lifted.

release time

The time it takes for a dynamics-processing device to change gain when the input signal crosses the threshold level while decreasing.

release velocity

The speed with which a key is raised and the type of MIDI data used to encode that speed. Release-velocity sensing is found on some instruments, although it is rare. It's usually used to control the rate of the release segments of an envelope or envelopes.

remote

1. Short for *remote control*, a device with which an operator can control a tape machine some distance away. 2. The recording taken at the site of a performance, rather than in a recording studio.

repeat echo

An echo effect caused by discrete repetitions of a program source by using a long delay time and feedback on a delay line. Also called *space echo*.

resonance

1. The prolonging of a sound at a certain frequency and the tendency of something to vibrate at a particular frequency after the source of energy is removed. 2. A function on a filter in which a narrow band of frequencies (the resonance peak) becomes relatively more prominent. If the resonance peak is high enough, the filter will begin to oscillate and produce an audio output, even in the absence of input. Filter resonance is also known as *emphasis and Q*, and on some older instruments is also known as *regeneration* or *feedback* (because feedback was used in the circuit to produce a resonance peak).

resonant

1. Term used to describe equipment that tends to pass signals of a certain frequency or narrow range of frequencies more than signals of other frequencies. 2. Physical properties that tend to reinforce the energy at certain frequencies of vibration are described as being resonant.

resonant frequency

The frequency at which a physical item tends to vibrate after the source of energy (which causes the vibration) is removed.

resonate

1. To vibrate at the resonant frequency. 2. To linger on, as in reverberation. In this respect,

the term is used in terms of sound in a room or is used to describe a room or other area that produces reverberation with a long reverb time.

return

Short for *echo return* or *auxiliary return*, ie the input of a console which brings the effect signal back from an echo chamber or other reverberation device.

reverb

1. The persistence of a sound after the source stops emitting it. 2. A function on a filter in which a narrow band of frequencies (the resonance peak) becomes relatively more prominent. If the resonance peak is high enough, the filter will begin to oscillate and produce an audio output, even in the absence of input. Filter resonance is also known as *emphasis and Q*, and on some older instruments is also known as *regeneration* or *feedback* (because feedback was used in the circuit to produce a resonance peak).

reverb(eration) time

The time it takes for the reverberation or echoes of a sound source to decrease by 60dB after the direct sound from the source stops.

reverberant field

The area away from a sound source at which reverberation is louder than the direct sound from the sound source.

reverberation envelope

Literally, the attack, decay, sustain and release of the reverberation volume. In other words, the time it takes for the reverberation to reach its peak level and its rate of decay. (See also *ADSR*.)

reverb-time contour

A graph of reverberation time for signals of different audio frequencies.

ribbon microphone

A microphone with a thin, conductive ribbon as both the diaphragm and the generating element (the device that generates the electricity).

riding the faders

The process of moving the faders up at quiet passages so that the signal will be recorded well above the noise and taking the faders back down during loud passages in order to prevent distortion.

riff

A short melody repeatedly played in a tune, sometimes with variation and often between vocal lines.

ringing

An undesirable resonance at the cut-off frequency of a filter that has a high rate of cut-off.

roll-off

The reduction of signal level as a signal's frequency moves away from the cut-off frequency, especially when the cut-off rate is mild.

room equalisation

An equaliser inserted in a monitor system that attempts to compensate for changes in frequency response caused by the acoustics of a room.

room sound

The ambience of a room, including reverberation and background noise.

room tone

The background noise in a room where there are no people speaking and there is no music playing.

rotary control

A level or other control in a device that has a circular movement rather than a linear movement.

round sound

A pleasingly balanced sound, ie one that has a pleasing mixture of high-frequency to low-frequency content.

RT

Abbreviation of *reverb time*, ie the time it takes for the reverberation or echoes of a sound source to decrease by 60dB after the direct sound from the source stops.

rumble

A low-frequency noise, especially that caused by earth/floor vibration or by uneven surfaces in the drive mechanism of a recorder or playback unit.

sample

1. In digital recording, to measure the level of a waveform at a given instant. 2. To record a short segment of audio for the purpose of playback later. 3. The short recording made in definition 2.

sample and hold

1. In digital recording, a term used to describe the measuring of the level of a waveform at a given instant and then converting it to a voltage at that level, which will then be held until another sample is taken. When triggered (usually by a clock pulse), a circuit on an analogue synthesiser looks at (samples) the voltage at its input and then passes it on to its output

unchanged, regardless of what the input voltage does in the meantime (the hold period), until the next trigger is received. In one familiar application, the input was a noise source and the output was connected to oscillator pitch, which caused the pitch to change in a random staircase pattern. The sample-and-hold effect is often emulated by digital synthesisers through an LFO waveshape called 'random'.

sample dump

The copying of a digitally recorded sample without converting it to analogue between different storage units or sound modules through a MIDI transmission.

sample playback

The reproduction (in analogue signal form) of a recorded sample, the pitch and sustain of which is controlled by a MIDI signal.

sampler

A device that records and plays samples, often including features for the editing and storage of the samples, usually by allowing them to be distributed across a keyboard and played back at various pitches.

sample rate

In digital recording, this term refers to the number of times that samples are taken each second.

sample-rate conversion

The conversion of digital audio data at one sample rate to digital audio data at a different sample rate without first converting the signal to analogue.

sampling

The process of encoding an analogue signal in digital form by reading (sampling) its level at precisely spaced time intervals.

sampling frequency

The same as *sample rate*, ie the number samples taken each second. Typical sampling rates are usually between 11kHz and 48kHz.

sampling synchronisation signal

A stream of synchronisation pulses that are generated by a digital audio tape recorder, recorded onto tape and then used as a clock signal to time the sampling of the sampling circuits.

sawtooth waveform

A waveform that jumps from a zero value to a peak value and then gradually diminishes to a zero value to complete the cycle.

scratch

1. A descriptive term meaning 'temporary'. 2. A scratch vocal is taken during a basic recording session to help the other musicians play their parts. At a later date, the final vocal track is overdubbed. 3. The action of a musician or disc jockey quickly moving a record back and forth with a phono cartridge reproducing the stylus motion in order to create a rhythmic pattern of sound.

scrub

1. To shuttle (ie move the sound track) either forward or backward when a control is moved off a centre point either left or right. 2. To move backward and forward through an audio waveform under manual control in order to find a precise point in a wave (for editing purposes).

SCSI

Abbreviation of *small-computer systems interface*, a high-speed communications protocol that allows computers, samplers and disk drives to communicate with one another. Pronounced 'scuzzy'.

SDS

The standard MIDI sample dump. SDS is used to transfer digital audio samples from one instrument to another over a MIDI cable.

send

A control and bus designed to feed signals from console channels to an outboard device, such as a reverberation unit.

send level

A control determining the signal level sent to a send bus.

separation

A term used to describe the pick-up of a desired signal compared to that of an undesired signal.

sequence

1. An automatic playing of musical events (such as pitches, sounding of samples and rests) by a device in a step-by-step order. 2. The action of programming a computer to play musical events automatically, in a stepped order.

sequencer

1. A computer which can be programmed to play and record a stepped order of musical events. 2. A device or program that records and plays back user-determined sets of music-performance commands, usually in the form of MIDI data. Most sequencers also allow this data to be edited in various ways and stored on disk.

set-up

An arrangement where microphones, instruments and controls on recorders, consoles, etc, are positioned for recording.

shield

1. The outer, conductive wrapping around an inner wire or wires in a cable. 2. To protect the inner wire or wires in a cable from picking up energy given off by such things as fluorescent lights.

shock mount

An elastic microphone mount that reduces the microphone's movement when the stand vibrates in response to floor vibrations from footsteps, etc.

short delay

Delay times under 20ms.

shortest digital path

The routing of a digital-audio signal so that there is a minimum amount of digital-to-analogue, analogue-to-digital or sample-rate conversion.

shortest path

A technique in recording by which a signal is routed through the least amount of active (amplified) devices during recording.

shotgun microphone

A microphone with a long line filter (a tube that acoustically cancels sound arriving from the side), thus allowing the microphone to pick up sound in one direction much better than in any other direction.

sibilance

Energy from a voice centred at around 7kHz, caused by pronouncing 's', 'sh' or 'ch' sounds.

signal processing

Changing the sound of an instrument or some other sound source with equalisers, limiters, compressors and other devices, thereby 'processing' the sound ready to be recorded onto a master.

signal-to-error ratio

The difference in level between the signal and the noise and distortion caused by converting analogue audio signals into digital audio and then back into analogue.

signal-to-noise ratio

The difference in decibels between the levels of signal and noise.

sine wave

The waveform produced by a sound source vibrating at one frequency (ie making a pure tone).

single D

Abbreviation of *single port distance*, used to describe a microphone in which there is one distance between the port and the diaphragm.

Single-Step mode

A method of loading events (such as notes) into memory one event at a time. Also called *step mode* and *step time*, compared with real time.

slap echo

One distinct repeat added to one or more instrument sounds in a mix that creates a very live sound, similar to what you'd hear in an arena.

slide

A control that has a knob which moves in a straight line and which outputs part of an input voltage according to the position of the knob.

smart FSK

An FSK (Frequency Shift Key) sync signal where the beginning of each measure has an identification message giving the measure number.

SMDI

Abbreviation of *SCSI musical data interchange*, a specification for sending MIDI sample dumps over the SCSI bus.

SMPTE

1. Society of Motion Picture and Television Engineers, a professional society. 2. A term loosely used to mean *SMPTE time code*, a standardised timing and sync signal specified by the aforementioned society.

SND

Sound resource, a Macintosh audio file format.

soft key

Abbreviation of *software key*, another name for a function key (ie a key that has a different function depending on the programming of a computer and as shown on a menu screen), especially when it's on a device that has an internal computer.

soft knob

Abbreviation of *software knob*, a knob used in a computer-controlled device which has a different function depending on the programming of the computer.

soft sound source

A low-volume instrument, such as an acoustic guitar.

solo

1. A circuit in a console that allows just one channel (or several selected channels) to be heard or reach the output. 2. In music, an instrument or section where an instrument is the featured instrument for a short period, often playing a melody. 3. An original Copy Code (protective digital signal recorded with digital audio bits) that was developed by Philips to prevent the making of digital copies of a copy made from a CD, thereby helping to prevent bootlegging.

solo switch

A switch that activates the solo function, which allows only selected channels to be heard or to reach the output.

song position pointer

1. Short for *MIDI clock with song pointer*, ie the time data contained in the MIDI signal used to sync two sequencers together. The song position pointer advances one step each $1/24$ of a beat, and also has a number signal for each measure or bar which indicates the number of measures or bars you are into the tune. 2. A type of MIDI data that tells a device how many 16th-notes have passed since the beginning of a song. An SPP message is generally sent in conjunction with a MIDI Continue message in order to start playback from the middle of a song.

sostenuto pedal

A pedal found on grand pianos and mimicked on some synthesisers, which only sustain notes if they are already being held down on the keyboard at the moment when the pedal is pressed.

sound absorption

The same as *acoustical absorption*, ie the quality of a surface or substance which takes in a sound wave rather than reflecting it.

sound card

A circuit board that is installed inside a computer (typically an IBM-compatible machine) providing new sound capabilities. These capabilities can include an FM or wavetable synthesiser and audio inputs and outputs. MIDI inputs and outputs are also normally included.

sound module

The signal-generator portion of a synthesiser or a sample playback unit that sends out an audio signal according to incoming MIDI messages and does not have keys with which to be played.

sound quality

A characteristic of how well the diaphragm movement in a microphone matches the pressure changes of a sound wave reaching it, particularly sudden changes.

sound wave

Abbreviation of *sound-pressure wave*, ie a wave of pressure changes moving away from something that is vibrating between 20 and 20,000 times a second.

spaced cardioid pair

A far-distant miking technique of placing two cardioid microphones a distance apart (usually about six inches) and pointing away from each other by 90 degrees.

spaced omni pair

Placing two microphones with omni-directional patterns between four and eight feet apart, so that one microphone picks up sound coming from the left and the other from the right.

space echo

An effect of repeating echoes of a sound.

SPDIF

Shortened from the first letters of Sony/Philips Digital Interface, a standard for sending and receiving digital audio signals using the common RCA connector.

split keyboard

A single keyboard divided electronically so that it acts as if it were two or more separate keyboards. The output of each note range is routed into a separate signal path in the keyboard's internal sound-producing circuitr, or transmitted over one or more separate MIDI channels. Applications include playing a bass sound with the left hand while playing a piano sound with the right.

spring reverb

A device that simulates reverberation by driving a spring (in the same way that a loudspeaker cone is driven) and picking up the spring's vibrations with a contact microphone (a device that converts physical vibrations into audio signals).

square wave

A wave shape produced when voltage rises instantly to one level, stays at that level, instantly falls to another level and stays at that level, and finally rises back to its original level to complete the cycle.

standing wave

An acoustic signal between two reflective surfaces with a distance that is an even multiple of half of the signal's frequency wavelength.

status byte

A MIDI byte that defines the meaning of the data bytes that follow it. MIDI status bytes always begin with a one (hex eight through to F), while data bytes always begin with a zero (hex zero through to seven).

step input

In sequencing, a technique that allows you to enter notes one step at a time, also called *step recording*. Common step values are 16th- and eighth-notes. After each entry, the sequencer's clock (ie its position in the sequence) will advance one step and then stop, awaiting new input. Recording while the clock is running is called *real-time input*.

step program/mode/time

To program a sequencer one note (or event) at a time in accordance with the rhythm to which the time value of one step is set.

stereo

A recording or reproduction of at least two channels where the positions of instrument sounds from left to right can be perceived.

stereo image

The perception of different sound sources being far left, far right or any place in between.

stereo miking

The positioning of two or more microphones in such a way that their outputs generate a stereo image.

stretched-string instruments

Instruments that use stretched strings to generate tones, such as guitars, violins and pianos.

subcode

Control information bits that are recorded along with digital audio and can be used for control of the playback deck, including functions such as program numbers, start IDs and skip IDs.

subframe

A unit smaller than one frame in SMPTE time code.

submaster

The fader that controls the level of sound from several channels (although not usually all channels) during mixdown or recording.

submix

A combination of audio signals treated as one or two channels (for a stereo image) in a mix.

subtractive synthesis

The generation of harmonically rich waveforms by various methods and then the filtering of these waveforms in order to remove unwanted harmonics and thus create sound. Alternatively, the technique of arriving at a desired tone colour by filtering waveforms rich in harmonics. Subtractive synthesis is the type generally used on analogue synthesisers.

super-cardioid pattern

A mic pattern that has maximum sensitivity on axis and least sensitivity around 150 degrees off axis.

surround sound

A technique of recording and playing back sound used in film, where the sound has a front-to-back quality as well as a side-to-side perspective.

sustain

1. A holding-out of the sounding of a pitch by an instrument. 2. The level at which a sound will continue to play when a synthesiser key is held down.

sustain pedal

The electronic equivalent of a piano's *sostenuto* (damper) pedal. In most synthesisers, the sustain pedal latches the envelopes of any currently playing or subsequently played notes at their sustain levels, even if the keys are lifted.

sweetening

Musical parts that are overdubbed in order to complete the music of a recording, especially the melodic instruments, such as strings and horns.

switchable-pattern microphone

A mic that has more than one directional pattern, depending on the Pattern switch's position.

sync box

A device that takes several different kinds of sync signals and puts out several kinds of sync signal, allowing a device such as a sequencer to be driven by a sync signal that it doesn't recognise.

synchronisation

The running of two devices in time with each other so that the events generated by each of them will always fall into predicable time relationships.

synthesiser

A musical instrument that artificially generates signals (using oscillators) to simulate the sounds of real instruments or to create other sounds impossible to manufacture with 'real' instruments and is designed according to certain principles developed by Robert Moog and others in the 1960s. A synthesiser is distinguished from an electronic piano or electronic organ by the fact that its sounds can be programmed by the user, and from a sampler by the fact that the sampler allows the user to make digital recordings of external sound sources.

system common

A type of MIDI data used to control certain aspects of the operation of an entire MIDI system.

System-common messages include Song Position Pointer messages, as well as Song Select, Tune Request, and End Of System Exclusive messages.

system exclusive (sysex)

A type of MIDI data that allows messages to be sent over a MIDI cable, which will then be responded to only by devices of a specific type. Sysex data is used most commonly for sending patch parameter data to and from an editor/librarian program.

system-exclusive bulk dump

A system-exclusive bulk dump is the transmission of internal synthesiser settings as a manufacturer-specified system-exclusive file from a synth to a sequencer or from a sequencer to a synth.

system real time

A type of MIDI data used for timing references. Because of its timing-critical nature, a system real-time byte can be inserted into the middle of any multibyte MIDI message. System real-time messages include MIDI Clock, Start, Stop, Continue, Active Sensing, and System Reset messages.

take

A recording taken between one start and the following stop of a track.

talk box

A guitar effects unit that allows a voice to modulate (control) a guitar signal. Operated by a vocalist talking with a tube in his mouth.

tempo

The rate at which the music progresses, measured in beats per minute (ie the number of steady, even pulses that occur in each minute of the music).

thin sound

A sound that doesn't have all frequencies present. Especially refers to a sound that is deficient in low frequencies.

three-to-one rule

The rule which states that the distance between microphones must be at least three times the distance between either microphone and the sound source.

Thru box

A unit with one MIDI In port and several MIDI Out ports. Each MIDI Out port has the same signal as the MIDI In port, but with a delay of the signal (usually around 4ms).

Thru port

A connector that puts out a MIDI signal identical to the input MIDI signal.

timbre

1. The timbre of the instrument is what makes it sound like that particular instrument and not like any other, even though the other instrument may be playing the same pitch. 2. One of the building blocks of a patch in a Roland synthesiser. Pronounced 'tam-br'.

time base

The number of pulses/advances per beat in a simple clock signal.

time code

Short for *SMPTE time code*, a standardised timing and sync signal specified by the Society of Motion Picture and Television Engineers. Alternatively, a type of signal that contains information about location in time and used for a synchronisation reference point when synchronising two or more machines together, such as sequencers, drum machines and tape decks.

time compression/expansion

The speeding up or slowing down of an audio recording without consequently changing the pitch.

timing clock

1. An even pulse signal used for syncing purposes. 2. The same as MIDI Clock, ie time data in a MIDI signal that advances one step each $1/24$ of a beat and can be used to sync two sequencers together.

tone

1. One of several single-frequency signals found at the beginning of a tape reel at the magnetic reference level that will be used to record a program. 2. Any single-frequency signal or sound. 3. The sound quality of an instrument's sound relative to the amount of energy present at different frequencies. 4. In some synthesisers, a term meaning the audio signal that will be put out by the unit which would be similar to the sound of an instrument.

touch sensitive

Used to describe a synthesiser keyboard's ability to generate a MIDI Velocity signal. Not all synthesiser keyboards are touch sensitive.

track

1. One audio recording made on a portion of the width of a multitrack tape. 2. One set of control commands in a sequencer recorded in a similar manner to an audio track and often controlling one synthesiser over one MIDI channel. 3. A term with the same meaning as the term *band track* (ie the part of a song without the lead vocal or without the lead and background vocals). 4. To be controlled by or to follow in some proportional relationship, such as when a filter's cut-off frequency tracks the keyboard, moving up or down depending on the note being played.

tracking

Recording the individual tracks of a multitrack recording.

transient

The initial high-energy peak that occurs at the beginning of a waveform, such as one caused by the percussive action of a pick or hammer hitting a string.

transient response

Response to signals with amplitudes which rise very quickly, such as drum beats and waveforms produced by percussive instruments.

transmit

In MIDI, to send a MIDI command to another device.

transposing

The act of changing the musical register of an entire piece of music by the space of an interval.

trap

A filter designed to reject audio signals at certain frequencies.

tremolo

An even, repeated change in volume of a musical tone. A periodic change in amplitude, usually controlled by an LFO, with a periodicity of less than 20Hz.

trigger

1. The signal or action of sending a signal to control the start of an event. 2. A device that emits a signal to control the start of an event, including a device that puts out such a signal when struck.

trim control

A device that reduces the strength of a signal produced by an amplifier, often over a restricted range.

trim status

Solid State Logic's Console Automation mode, which operates as follows: when a slide is at its trim point, the gain variations (fader movements) last programmed in the computer will be in effect; when the slide is moved from the trim point, gain or loss is added to or subtracted from the program.

tuned

A term used with reference to a circuit or device which is most sensitive to a certain frequency.

tweak

A slang term meaning to calibrate (ie to set all operating controls and adjustments in order to obtain a device's optimum performance), particularly in terms of very precise calibration.

unidirectional

A pick-up pattern that's more sensitive to sound arriving from one direction than from any other.

unison

Several performers, instruments or sound sources sounding at the same time and with the same pitch.

vamp

The repeated part of a tune at its end, usually the chorus or part of the chorus.

Variable-D

A patented invention of Electrovoice where several ports are inserted in the casing of a microphone. These ports are increasingly less sensitive to high frequencies, as they are further away from the diaphragm, reducing the proximity effect.

velocity

In synthesisers and keyboard controllers, a MIDI message giving data on how hard a key is struck. Alternatively, a type of MIDI data (ranging between 1 and 127) usually used to indicate how quickly a key is pushed down (attack velocity) or allowed to rise (release velocity). (A Note-On message with a velocity value of zero is equivalent to a Note-Off message.)

velocity curve

A map that translates incoming velocity values into other velocities in order to alter the feel or response of a keyboard or tone module.

velocity microphone

Another name for *pressure-gradient microphone*, ie one whose diaphragm is exposed at the front and back and the movement of which is caused by small differences in pressure between the front and back of the diaphragm.

velocity sensitive

The same as *touch sensitive*, used to describe a synthesiser keyboard's ability to generate a MIDI Velocity signal. Not all synthesiser keyboards are velocity sensitive.

vibrato

1. A smooth and repeated changing of pitch up and down from the regular musical pitch, often practised by singers. 2. A periodic change in frequency, often controlled by an LFO, with a periodicity of less than 20Hz.

virtual

Existing only in software.

virtual tracking

Having a MIDI sequencer operating in sync with a multitrack tape and controlling the playing of synthesisers along with recorded parts.

vocal booth

A isolation room used to record a vocal track so that other instruments in the studio don't leak into the vocal microphone. Also used to reduce ambience and reverberation in a vocal recording.

vocoder

An effects device that will modulate (control) one signal with another.

voice

1. In synthesisers, a pitch that can be played at the same time as other pitches. 2. In Yamaha synths, a term meaning the same thing as *sound patch*, ie a sound that can be created by the synth.

voice channel

A signal path containing (as a minimum) an oscillator and VCA, or their digital equivalent, and capable of producing a note. On a typical synthesiser, two or more voice channels - each with their own waveform and parameter settings - can be combined to form a single note.

voice stealing

A process by which a synth that is required to play more notes than it has available voices switches off some of the voices that are currently sounding (typically those that have been sounding the longest or are the lowest amplitude) in order to assign them to play new notes.

volume

1. A common, non-technical term equivalent to level of sound pressure and loosely applied to also mean audio voltage level. 2. Abbreviation of the term *volume control*.

volume control

An amplifier's gain control.

volume envelope

The way in which a note sounded by a musical instrument changes in volume over time.

volume pedal

A guitar pedal used to change the volume of an instrument or a similar device used with other instruments, such as an organ.

volume unit

A unit designed to measure perceived changes in loudness in audio material. The unit is basically the decibel change of the average level, as read by a volume unit (VU) meter. The movement of the VU meter is designed to approximately match the ear's response to changes in level.

VU

1. Abbreviation of the term *volume unit*, ie a unit designed to measure perceived changes in loudness in audio material. 2. A meter that reads levels of audio voltage fed into or out of a piece of equipment and is designed to match the ear's response to sudden changes in level.

wah/wah-wah

A changing filter that filters either more or less of an instrument's harmonics.

WAV

The Windows audio file format. Typically encountered as 'filename.wav'.

wave

A continuous fluctuation in the amplitude of a quantity with respect to time.

waveform/waveshape

The shape made by fluctuations in a wave over a period over time.

wavelength

The length of one cycle (in feet, inches, etc) of a wave.

wavetable synthesis

A common method for generating sound electronically on a synthesiser or PC. Output is produced using a table of sound samples (actual recorded sounds) which are digitised and played back as needed. By continuously re-reading samples and looping them together at different pitches, highly complex tones can be generated from a minimum of stored data without overtaxing the processor.

wave velocity

The time it takes for one point of a waveform to travel a certain distance.

wet

Having reverberation or ambience. Alternatively, consisting entirely of processed sound. The output of an effects device is 100 per cent wet when only the output of the processor itself is being heard, with none of the dry (unprocessed) signal.

wheel

A controller used for pitch bending or modulation, normally mounted on the left-hand side of the keyboard and played with the left hand.

white noise

Random energy distributed so that the amount of energy is the same for each cycle, causing the noise level to increase with frequency.

wide-band noise

Noise that has energy over a wide range of frequencies.

width

Another term for *depth*, ie the amount of change in a controlled signal exerted by the control signal.

wild sound

Sound recordings that are taken completely separately from the master recording (or *picture recording*), and therefore can't be synced to the master recording.

windscreen

A device that reduces or eliminates wind noise from the microphone being moved or from blowing into the microphone on remote-location recordings.

wireless microphone

A microphone with an FM radio transmitter inside its casing that transmits a signal to an offstage FM receiver.

woodwind controller

A device that plays like a woodwind instrument, controlling a sound module by putting out a control voltage or MIDI command.

XLR connector

1. A common three-pin connector used in balanced audio connections. 2. A microphone cable.

XY miking

A method of arranged two cardioid microphones for stereo pick-up, with the two mic heads positioned as close together as possible without touching, pointing 90 degrees away from each other and 45 degrees to the centre of the sound source.

Y-cord/lead

A cable fitted with three connectors, so that one output may be sent to two inputs.

zero-crossing point

The point at which a digitally encoded waveform crosses the centre of its amplitude range.